BLOOD & FIRE

The autobiography of the UB40 brothers

Ali and Robin Campbell were born and brought up in 1960's Birmingham and went on to lead one of pop/reggae music legends UB40 with records sales in excess of £50 million.

Paul Gorman is a London-based writer who has written for a wide variety of publications from the *Evening Standard*, the *Daily Telegraph* and the *Radio Times* to *heat* and *Mojo*.

Tim Abbot is a Midlands-based entrepreneur whose management and marketing track record includes Creation Records, Oasis, Robbie Williams, UB40 and Fatboy Slim.

Also available by Paul Gorman

The Look: Adventures in Pop & Rock Fashion
In Their Own Write
Nine Lives with Goldie
Straight with Boy George

Also available by Tim Abbott

Oasis: Definitely

ALI & ROBIN CAMPBELL

BLOOD & FIRE

The autobiography of the UB40 brothers

arrow books

Published in the United Kingdom by Arrow books in 2006

1 3 5 7 9 10 8 6 4 2

Copyright © Ali and Robin Campbell 2005

Ali and Robin Campbell have asserted their right under the Copyright, Designs
and Patents Act, 1988 to be identified as the authors of this work

First published in the United Kingdom in 2005 by Century

The Random House Group Limited
20 Vauxhall Bridge Road, London SW1V 2SA

Random House Australia (Pty) Limited
20 Alfred Street, Milsons Point, Sydney,
New South Wales 2061, Australia

Random House New Zealand Limited
18 Poland Road, Glenfield
Auckland 10, New Zealand

Random House (Pty) Limited
Isle of Houghton, Corner of Boundary Road & Carse O'Gowrie,
Houghton 2198, South Africa

The Random House Group Limited Reg. No. 954009

www.randomhouse.co.uk

A CIP catalogue record for this book is available
from the British Library

Papers used by Random House are
natural, recyclable products made from wood grown in
sustainable forests. The manufacturing processes conform to
the environmental regulations of the country of origin

ISBN 9780099476542 (from Jan 2007)
ISBN 0099476541

Printed and bound in Great Britain by
Bookmarque Ltd, Croydon, Surrey

To our family and
Raymond and Lloyd

Acknowledgements

Tim Abbot and Paul Gorman would like to thank the following for their assistance, patience and inspiration:

Carole Beirne, Lanval Storrod, Paul Hunter, Dave Parker and Danny Sprigg at DEP International; Simon Trewin and Claire Gill at PFD; Hannah Black, Victoria Hunt and Kevin Redmond at Century; Bill Curbishley and Cookie Brusa at Trinifold; Joris van Drunen Littel and Norman de Langen of the website 2-DuB (http://home.iae.nl/users/jjvdl/main.html); Chris Abbot (the Ras' With Class) and DC 666. Thanks to Jo Pestell.

Most of all we'd like to thank Ali and Rob for hours of mind-expanding enlightenment.

Introduction

The Brother Blend

Ali and Robin Campbell are, by their own admission, 'like chalk and cheese'. If you didn't know it, the fact of their brotherhood would, at least on cursory inspection, be difficult to discern.

One dapper and precise, forever dressed in black, darting around a snooker table or expertly discussing the comparative skills of boxing legends; the other laidback and slyly humorous, announcing his presence with a stream of one-liners to mask the shyness which adds to the wary air he exudes on first contact.

But watch them relax – in time-honoured and ubiquitous UB40-style, surrounded by wreaths of smoke – and the 'brother blend' emerges, that mixture of blood and fire where their shared passions for reggae, for justice, for multi-culturalism and equality are rarely far from the surface.

The brother blend is a musical term to denote the natural harmony of sibling voices, but it cuts deeper for these two, who, for a quarter of a century now, have conducted their relationship on sound stages from tiny Midlands pubs to Wembley Stadium and in recording studios, dressing rooms, hotels, bars and low dives the world over.

And that relationship has been tested to the limit, not least by the conflict created by Ali's appetites and Robin's relative asceticism.

Yet their fraternal bond has helped them overcome such problems and Ali and Robin combine as the axis on which the formidable reggae democracy of UB40 turns. They are at the centre of an extended family which encompasses partners and ex-wives, children and grandchildren, crew members of long-standing, employees at their nerve centre DEP and musical collaborators from Chrissie Hynde to Augustus Pablo.

This book, which took two-and-a-half years from conception to completion, has proved a revelation, undercutting the unfair portrait sometimes depicted in the media of the band, its members and their music. But this is not just the story of UB40; it is that of two brothers enriched and enlightened by their extraordinary experiences.

Maybe it's because Ali and Robin are embedded in a radical and musical heritage stretching back nearly a century that they have been able to handle circumstances which have crushed the careers of lesser artists.

From riots, police busts, corruption and bribery in every part of the globe to multi-million-pound financial calamities at home; from personal tribulations such as divorce and separation to betrayal and loss; from the damaging effects of drink and drugs to the fickleness of the music industry, all of these have taken their toll, but Ali and Robin are proof positive that the brother blend will out and blood and fire will see you through.

Paul Gorman/Tim Abbot
London/Walsall 2005

1

Ghetto Wonderland

Growing up in the 60s, our home was like none of the other council houses in Balsall Heath's red-light district in inner-city Birmingham.

While prostitutes prowled the streets, which throbbed to Motown and ska, bluebeat and reggae, our house was filled with a mix that couldn't have been more at odds with our immediate environment: traditional folk music, left-wing politics and rigorous Scottish values.

All of those came courtesy of our father, Ian, but in truth they stemmed from one man, our grandad, Dave Campbell, who brought the clan south from Aberdeen to the West Midlands after the end of the Second World War. Grandad was a very proud man, a staunch socialist, passionate trade unionist and all-round champion of the working man who had found himself in deep water back home. He had been getting up the noses of the bosses for years, organising the workers not just during the depression of the 30s but also in the grim post-war period of austerity and conservatism.

By the time he met our gran, Betty, in 1931, Dave Campbell

also had a reputation for singing the 'bothy ballads' of Aberdeen-shire. He came from a family of singers: his own father, uncle and three brothers were all known locally for their strong voices. The story goes that when they were courting, one of the first things Gran did was teach him a song, 'The Road to Dundee'. She had learnt it in a girls' club, and by teaching it to Grandad she ensured they could sing it as a duo. Our grandparents continued to sing that song together at public performances and private family parties throughout their lives and more than fifty years of marriage, God bless 'em.

In the early years of their marriage, Grandad was forced to leave his wife and home in Aberdeen and head out on the road in search of manual labour at harvest time, staying in the little stone huts known as bothies with up to ten men in each room, sleeping above the horses. Grandad used to tell us about how the only entertainment was the singing sessions, when each labourer would come up with old and new folk songs about life, love and hardship. With harvest over, Grandad would take his earnings and the songs back home with him, to the tiny tenement house where he lived with Gran and their kids: our aunties Lorna and Billie, our uncle David and our dad, Ian, who was born at the height of the depression in 1933. By that time Grandad had been involved in the unemployment movement for several years, undertaking hunger marches and speaking regularly at rallies to persuade the government to provide bearable living conditions for those who had been hit hardest by the slump.

But, so we've been told, they weren't all bad times. When the eating and drinking were over – the men got beer, the women were restricted to cups of tea! – the singing would start. In fact they were at it all the while; Grandad always said that singing on the marches was the greatest morale-booster of all.

Grandad arrived in the Midlands in 1946 with the rest of his family. To this day we're not sure what triggered the decision to move the family lock, stock and barrel, but we know that on at least one occasion he was badly beaten by the bully boys employed by the bosses and dock owners. The promise of work without such aggravation combined with a more agreeable atmosphere to practise his politics was bound to be a lure. Grandad – who worked in engineering and later at the dog track and on the door for the famous wrestling matches at Digbeth Civic Hall – had a forceful, domineering personality, and the family joke was always: 'When is Grandad going to ask, "Is it time for me to sing now?"'

It is a Campbell trait to be loud and opinionated, and maybe there is something of that in both of us as well. He certainly passed it on to our old man, who shared his father's fiercely held political convictions but took the family interest in traditional music to a new level.

When they were in their late teens, Dad met our mom, Patricia Weaver from Great Barr. Known as Pat to everybody, her mother's side of the family came from Dorset, near to where Ali now lives, so he's kind of closed that family circle.

Mom and Dad met in 1951 when they were both 18. Mom was a member of the unity theatre when Dad and a mate came to borrow costumes for a YCL Christmas party. He invited her along. She went and fell for him there and then (in his great big Australian hat, she says), smitten by this working class, intellectual lefty and talented musician.

She then went along to a new year's eve party at his parents' house and they were married six months later.

Dad had been an apprentice printing engraver, which had deferred his national service, but marriage meant no apprentice-ship, so off he went to do his bit. Mom stayed at home and had David in January 1953, and Dad came home in September 1954, a few months before my birth, narrowly avoiding a stint in Korea.

'It's funny, but there's a picture of me at eighteen with quite long hair,' says Robin. 'There is also a photo of Mom at the same age and I look exactly like her! Dark hair and quite delicate features, whereas Ali, when he had the quiff in the 80s, looked the spit of our old man. The only difference between them is that Dad had a folky's beard, but the likeness in physique and looks is remarkable.'

We can see that we inherited similar personality traits from each parent as well. Mom is more reserved than Dad, who has always been a forthright and outgoing person. 'I tend to keep my own counsel, just like our mom,' says Robin. 'It's ironic that although Ali is essentially quite shy, he can also be extrovert and is very similar to our dad in many ways. Ali's been a great carouser in his time, just like the old man.'

Dad formed his first band when he was quite young. The skiffle craze which swept Britain in the late 50s opened the doors for many young musicians who didn't have to be that proficient at their instruments to make a racket. It was cheap to put a group together because all you needed was an acoustic guitar, a washboard and anything else that came to hand, including the kitchen broom.

But Dad wasn't into the American blues and roots music which dominated the skiffle scene. Out of the army and working as a metal engraver, Dad joined the Clarion Choir (a left-wing outfit run by Cath Thompson, wife of internationally renowned intellectual Professor George Thompson). But being musically ambitious he left to form a group of his own, with his sister Lorna. Though they had the briefest of flirtations with what our old man calls, 'The great skiffle disaster', Dad and Lorna's real interest was in Scottish and Irish traditional folk music. They formed the Ian Campbell Folk Group in 1958 and went on to be founders and leading lights of the 'British Folk Music Revival'.

Our house was pretty crowded: there are four of us brothers – the eldest, David, was born in 1953, Robin came along on Christmas Day 1954, Duncan is three and a half years younger and Ali arrived just ten months after him, in 1959.

'When I was just a nipper we lived at 88 Albion Street in

Hockley, over a shop in the yard which belonged to the factory that employed the old man as an engraver,' says Robin. 'It was that close he could jump over the wall to go to work every morning, and jump back once he had finished in the evening. That was his day job but his hobby at nights and at weekends was playing folk in the clubs that were springing up locally as well as all over the country at that time.'

Ali remembers being carried by our mom as she handed Dad his lunch over the wall. 'I can only have been about three. My memories are black and white; where we lived was like a tenement yard,' he says. 'I can remember our parents arguing and Mom crying. I also well remember setting fire to the shed in the yard!'

Our cat Mac spent more time in the factory than he did in our house. The moggy would be over there ratting, and when he had finished his killing spree, would proudly line up the dead prey on the wall for us to inspect. He went feral in the end.

Albion Street was real tenement living, but in the early 60s, when the Ian Campbell Folk Group started to take off, Dad gave up his day job and became a professional musician. That was when we moved to Balsall Heath, opposite Calthorpe Park at 25 Speedwell Road.

Balsall Heath was a scruffy area on the edges of prosperous Edgbaston. As well as the seedy elements and immigrant culture, it also had bohemian, arty associations. The Birmingham branch of the British Surrealist Movement had actually been founded at the house right next door to ours, number 23. Speedwell Road was between Varna Road and Alexandra Road, which put us slap bang in the red-light district. When we were growing up, we'd run errands for the prostitutes in the area, going to buy them fags, condoms and other groceries. In return they'd give us a few bob or a couple of cigarettes.

It's strange to think now, but this was still pre-Beatles, and there really was a huge folk boom. Dad's group had become a pretty big deal, playing to full houses at places like the Royal Albert

Hall and the Royal Festival Hall. Dad was, and still is, a very talented musician and singer/songwriter. Among the highpoints of his career was his twelve-song suite called *Adam's Rib*, which he wrote for Lorna about the different crisis points in a woman's life.

The Ian Campbell Folk Group recorded more than twenty albums, as well as EPs like *Songs of Protest* and *Ceilidh at the Crown*, which was the first-ever live folk group recording to be released. And some of the other members went on to carve out names for themselves, like the fiddler Dave Swarbrick, who formed Fairport Convention with one of the Ian Campbell Folk Group bass players, Dave Pegg, who was in Jethro Tull.

Dad's song 'The Sun is Burning' became the official theme of the Campaign for Nuclear Disarmament at the time. There's plenty of news footage of thousands of demonstrators singing it on marches and at rallies at Trafalgar Square and Aldermaston in the early 60s. As little kids we went on the marches, singing 'We Shall Overcome' as we were hoisted onto the shoulders of our parents and their friends.

Dad came very close to big-time success himself when Simon & Garfunkel recorded 'The Sun is Burning' for the *Bridge Over Troubled Water* album. Then, at the last minute, they decided against including it in the final track listing. That album sold millions of copies, and our dad would have received worldwide recognition for his songwriting talent. But maybe it was for the best; the success would probably have killed the old man, since he would have felt so guilty about earning all that money!

Dad is a brilliant songwriter, particularly clever when it comes to lyrics. 'Tracks of his like "The Sun is Burning", "Across the Hills", "Come Kiss Me Love" – they are all great songs,' says Robin.

The Ian Campbell Folk Group scored a real breakthrough for British folkies when they were invited to play in the US, at the Newport Folk Festival in 1964, but Dad's Communist Party membership caught up with him and the organisers couldn't obtain permission for him to enter the country. Still, his group became the first non-Americans to record Dylan's 'The Times They Are A-Changin'', which also became a staple on the protest marches. The Ian Campbell Folk Group's version even got Dad into the charts at number 50, but just as it was making some headway CBS released the Dylan original, which blew Dad's out of the water.

For many years Dad ran Europe's biggest folk club, the Jug O' Punch, at Digbeth Civic Hall, which also hosted the famous wrestling bouts televised every Saturday afternoon, featuring the likes of Mick McManus and Jackie Pallo.

Grandad took the tickets on the door of the Jug, which was played by everyone on the folk scene, from Joni Mitchell and Paul Simon to Billy Connolly – when he was playing banjo and guitar solo as well as with his early group, the Humblebums. 'Billy was another refugee from the Great Skiffle Disaster, but became a comedian by cracking jokes and telling stories to keep the crowds entertained in-between songs,' says Robin. Among the other regular performers at the Jug were the Dubliners, whose mainman, Ronnie Drew, still comes to our gigs whenever we play Dublin. 'I remember walking up to our house as a kid and Ronnie was standing there pissing out of the front door,' smiles Ali. 'He looked at me and said, "Oh, I thought this was the back door," and went off and continued slashing out there.'

Just like us and reggae much later on, Dad and his pals were on a mission to popularise the music they loved. It was only afterwards they realised that traditional folk music had never really been of great fascination to the working classes and was a minority interest at best. When they took their music to the working-men's institutes and clubs they found that people wanted to play dominoes and darts, and weren't the slightest bit impressed by a bunch of folkies standing around warbling away with hands cupped to their ears in the traditional style.

But among students and music fans, folk was huge for a while. Us kids well remember going to the Jug as toddlers, taking in all the antics of these strange and interesting people with their beards and long hair – and that was just the women! The musicians who played there would often stay over at our house and many's the morning we'd come down for breakfast before school and find a shabby folk singer asleep on the settee.

Because Dad was often on the road or hosting the club, we were used to hearing from professional musicians about the business; that was to stand us in good stead much later on.

The old man knew everybody who had worked the folk and blues circuit. When Long John Baldry went to number one with 'Let the Heartaches Begin' in 1967, he came to Birmingham and did his act, which was by then sophisticated pop, with him in a tux and all. John had organised some tickets for Mom and Dad, who even wore a suit that night. Ali simply didn't believe that they knew somebody who was at number one in the charts, so Dad returned with a programme on which Baldry had written: 'To Ali. I know your Dad!'

We travelled around the country with Dad to gigs and folk festivals, and even got the chance to go further afield. 'I went on a tour of Scotland with him, and another time flew with him to Czechoslavakia,' says Robin. 'Because the Communist Party had invited him, there was no money in it, but they offered an extra free flight, so he grabbed the opportunity to take me because it was during the school holidays.'

We spent a lot of evenings at the Jug. Actually, it was the place where Ali made his stage debut, at the age of eight, with Dave Swarbrick's daughter Suss, singing 'Why Does It Have to Be Me?' A few years later, when he was thirteen, Ali, Duncan, Ali's mate Norman Hassan – who lived down the road and later formed UB40 with us – and Norman's sister Maria performed an a cappella version of an Arabic song, 'Ya Mustapha', and, believe it or not, 'You Are My Sunshine'!

Dad appeared regularly on the telly when we were growing up, on programmes with titles like the *Hootenanny Show* and *Barn Dance*, but like any self-respecting folk singer he was pretty scruffy. 'He always wore crap clothes as far as I was concerned,' says Ali. 'He may have been on telly but he was never hip, always wearing the stuff he'd walk around the house in, baggy unironed jeans. I'd think: Make a bit of an effort Dad! But he was a folk singer, and the last thing on his mind was showbiz presentation.'

He was also a regular on local television shows like *Midlands Today* and *High Tea*, which went out at four o'clock every afternoon, hosted by Noele Gordon, later Meg Richardson of *Crossroads* fame. 'I clearly remember watching him on *High Tea* when I was about seven, doing a happy-clappy folk song,' says Robin. 'In fact, he was such a local face around that time that people wouldn't believe he was my dad. We were proud of him and it did make a difference, seeing him perform and getting tickets for the shows which came to town. We were never ashamed, but my mates thought I was lying when I told them who he was.

'"What do you mean?" they'd say. "He can't be your father. You live in a council house in Balsall Heath and he's on the telly every week!" Eventually it was easier to say my father was a dustbinman. That would end the conversation.'

2

Father

Our old man insisted we live in a council house because his socialist principles wouldn't allow him to own property: he strongly believed that it was an evil manifestation of materialism. Even when we eventually moved into our own house in the late 60s, the mortgage was in our mother's name because he was so against it.

'I suppose Robin and I were the closest when we were kids,' says Ali. 'Sometimes we'd gang up on the other two. Duncan, Robin and I shared a room and Dave had one to himself. He was a right hippy at the time, walking around the house in the nude with a top hat on and all this long hair. Dad would say, "Are you going to do that all day long?" He'd answer, "Yeah." Dad would shake his head in resigned annoyance.'

David would think nothing of it. He was truly proud of his dick, which would dangle down for all to see. From the age of twelve he'd be going: 'Look at that. Not bad eh?' It would take one of our parents to say reprovingly, 'Dave. . .' and he'd apologise and go and put some trousers on.

Dave didn't smoke joints at home but was thrown out of school not only for smoking one in the headmaster's personal toilet but also for lighting his joss sticks in the school chapel during the Friday service.

Even though David was only two years older than Robin and went to the same secondary school, he always seemed to be more grown up than us. He was six-foot tall at the age of twelve, which is also when he started shaving. Compared to him, the rest of us brothers were babies, which is maybe why the three of us formed a bit of a gang between us.

'David was much more mature than us, and there were other differences: he couldn't ride a bike and wasn't interested in football, so Ali, Duncan and I would be over in the park with all our mates while he was off with his own crew,' says Robin.

Dave and Robin served time in the Woodcraft Folk, the organisation for the kids of socialists who weren't allowed to join the Scouts because of its quasi-military leanings. In fact Robin's first media appearance was on the front page of the Birmingham *Evening Mail* – complete with a photo of him peeling potatoes – because he was the youngest ever Woodcraft Folk member at six and a half. The entry age was actually eight, but they bent the rules because David was already a member and, after all, Dad was Ian Campbell.

The adults around us were very hard-line politically. In fact our Aunt Lorna still speaks from that kind of viewpoint: 'We don't like this', or: 'We approve of that.' Our mom also has strong political convictions but because of her nature was always less outspoken than the Campbells. And, when Dad was on tour with Lorna and the rest of his band, Mom was stuck at home raising four kids. Many times people mistook mom for Lorna and vice versa.

The average teatime when Dad was away would be riotous. There'd be all of us and usually a couple of our friends sat at the table, and the jokes and chat would flow. Ali in particular would bring his pals, kids such as Norman and Jimmy Brown, Brian Travers and Earl Falconer, all of whom later formed UB40 with us.

When Dad was at home tea tended to be a much more silent

affair. If he was in the mood we'd have a great time, but if he wasn't, silence was required. One mealtime our friend Dexter Brown joined us, and we ate with our food on our laps. Dad strode into the sitting room with his plate in his hand and, without looking at anyone, changed the TV channel. Then he went to sit down but misjudged the chair, tilted backwards and tipped his plate of spag-bol all over his face. As he rocked forward, it came splashing back into his plate. There was a silence of about five seconds as we all looked for Dad's reaction, and then Dexter burst out laughing and the tension was broken.

Things were more relaxed with Dad on the nights of gigs at The Jug, when he would come home late with his pals and some stragglers from the club, very merry and bringing Chinese or Indian food which would be shared out to us kids; those were the nights we were allowed to stay up until midnight.

That was great, eating food from other cultures. Because of the way our dad lived, we were opened up to new experiences early in life, such as being taken out for baltis before they really became established in this country. From a young age we'd be eating chapatis and nans at places like Bhutt's and Imran's on Ladypool Road, the first to sell that kind of food. The owner of Bhutt's was a championship wrestler who's dead now, but both restaurants are still there and we still go regularly. They were the only ones in Brum at the time; these days that area is known as the Balti Belt because there are two hundred just in that neighbourhood.

When we were growing up, our area was a real melting pot, to say the least. The kid next door was black, the kid on the other side was Arabic, the kid across the road was a Pakistani.

It was natural that we should get to know everybody and share cultures. Balsall Heath was a fantastic place to be as a child but the atmosphere in our house depended very much on whether Dad was there or not, because he was so often away on tour.

If our dad was in a good mood – which wasn't often enough – he could be great fun, telling stories and making us laugh. He's a great raconteur, talking about life on the road and other cultures. He'd bring home instruments which he'd try to teach us to play – such as the Irish drum, the bodhrán – and was constantly on at us to learn the penny whistle or the Jew's harp, anything folky. And Dad made his own instruments: one time he even constructed a square banjo. Years later Ali commissioned the first (and possibly only!) Banjocaster – local guitar-maker John Diggins put a banjo neck on a Stratocaster for him. The Banjocaster has yet to feature on one of our records, but appeared in the Maybe Tomorrow video.

Way back when, at the age of twelve, Robin innocently asked about playing the guitar, and Dad immediately had his own guitar player, Brian Clark – who was married to Lorna – giving him lessons.

One day when we were all in our teens, Mom decided to stop going to the Jug on Thursday nights; great news for us because it meant we stayed with her, watching programmes we liked, like *The Untouchables*, while he was out. Dad could be a bit of a tyrant. He drank a lot and would sometimes become unpleasant or argumentative after he'd had a few, very fierce and acerbic.

Once, when Duncan was in his teens, he cooked us all a spaghetti bolognese and, unfortunately for him, the old man arrived home pissed just before dinnertime. Having lovingly prepared the meal, Duncan sprinkled it with Parmesan, and when it was served the old man went mad about the smell: 'This is disgusting! Your feet stink! Get out!' And, all because of a bit of grated cheese, Duncan was physically ejected from the room.

Dad could also be very thoughtless. If one of the boys had a girl round and was trying to impress her, he'd do his best to humiliate us. Ali can remember being lifted bodily out of his chair in front of a new girlfriend: 'That's my chair: Off!'

There would be so many similar stupid actions which would annoy us. For years on end Dad made a big thing about buying a packet of biscuits and eating all of them in front of us as we watched telly. You'd ask for one and he'd refuse. Not even our mom was allowed a single biscuit. So, one day – after he had left home, he'd never have dared do this before – Robin brought round his own packet and offered them around to everyone but the old man. He sat there silently trying to keep a straight face. 'I had to do pathetic things like that to get the message across', says Robin.

We were always proud of Dad's achievements but he was absent for so much of the time it was inevitable that we didn't become as close to him as we were with our mom.

3

A Family Affair

Campbell family get-togethers were just like those all over Scotland, Ireland and anywhere else in the world where Celts and their descendants gather. Everyone – grandparents, aunties, uncles, nippers – would be expected to sing their own particular song. Out of us brothers, Duncan and Dave followed in the family tradition and developed a love for folk music. They liked the same music as us, but never abandoned things like the boozy Sunday folk-singing sessions.

Us two reacted differently to the drink-filled atmosphere of such gatherings. Ali traces the alcoholism which dogged him in later life back to the environment of our childhood.

'They say it's hereditary and both my grandad and father were alcoholics,' says Ali. 'I clearly remember being pissed on shandy at five years old as a page boy at the wedding of a family friend, Edmund Preston. By the age of eight or nine I was off to my dad's folk club drinking people's leftovers at the end of the night, or when everyone had gone from the Thursday nights at Speedwell Road I would clear the glasses out. We were encouraged to drink as kids: single-malt whisky or Athel brose at Hogmanay, that sort of thing.'

Robin, on the other hand, followed our mom in adopting a more sober approach. 'I've never felt comfortable around drunk people,' he says. 'I'd watched my dad and that whole side of the family drink too much and I didn't enjoy witnessing it as a kid, so as an adult I've never found it attractive. It would be the same-old, same-old. Maybe they'd be loving, or sometimes funny, but people would be repeating themselves, or become aggressive and boring. I wasn't an angel, and would pinch nips of the old man's scotch as a teenager, but would never reach the stage of becoming shit-faced. I don't like being out of control, like Ali did.'

This is where another similarity between Robin and our mom's personalities comes in. Our mom's not teetotal or anything, she'll have a drink and get merry, but she had a house to run and mouths to feed, getting the kids up for school in the morning, so very often she'd find herself in a roomful of people who were all flying when she wasn't.

'She will still go to the occasional family session,' says Robin, 'but that's more to do with keeping up with her ex-mother-in-law and others on me dad's side of the family. Very often she would sit back and let them get on with it, and I would do the same sort of thing, which could be quite lonely.'

Of our other brothers, Duncan still loves folk (and booze!) and plays the spoons professionally. You can find him in the Musicians' Union directory. Look under 'SP' for spoons and there he is: Duncan Sutherland Campbell. Anyone can play the spoons as well as Duncan but he wanted to get into the MU, so wrote on the form: 'Vocals and spoons.' Almost immediately he was asked by Radio 2 to play on a paid session.

David was always the most politically out there, infused with the radical ideas percolating out of the counterculture. Remember this was a very volatile time: the Angry Brigade was exploding bombs all over the country, strikes and walk-outs and sit-ins seemed to happen on a weekly basis, there were riots ending in death and tragedy in Northern Ireland and anti-Vietnam war demonstrations kicking off confrontations with the police virtually every week.

In fact, Ali, in an early political act, aged nine, daubed VIETNAM in red paint on the wall at the top of the stairs. 'I thought that they wouldn't know which of us had written it,' he says. 'Unfortunately I misspelt it VEITNAM, so they knew who was responsible as soon as I'd done it.'

David was a fan of the underground press and wrote for various subversive publications. He also involved himself in all manner of insurrectionary behaviour, but that came to a head in the mid-70s when he and his mates robbed a London bookie's in an anarchistic act in support of a fringe revolutionary movement. They used toy guns and were nicked immediately for attempted armed robbery. They had been spotted outside acting suspiciously and as soon as they had committed the act they were pinched.

'David's a very intelligent, articulate, gentle man,' says Robin. 'I can see Ali or me – if we hadn't become pop stars – or even Duncan for that matter becoming involved in robbery or turning into gangsters. We were on the fringes of petty crime all the time. But David was, and is, so far removed from that world I was completely dumbfounded by the whole affair.

Dave and his group were cerebral revolutionaries sitting around discussing how to change the world. Our parents were deeply shocked and upset. Dave and his mates certainly weren't hardened blaggers, but the authorities came down on them like a ton of bricks. They were defended by Tony Gifford, the radical barrister who is now Lord Gifford and handled such cases as the appeals by the Guildford Four and the Birmingham Six. Gifford was also Ken Livingstone's legal advisor during the GLC years and even set up the first Law Centre in the country. David was working for him as a clerk at the time of the robbery.

Maybe that's what did for them; having Gifford on your team was bound to have riled the establishment. The court certainly wasn't persuaded by the argument that the robbery had been

politically motivated and they were given the maximum sentence
of seven years and ended up serving more than four, at first in a
high-security jail. This was a very heavy experience for a young
lad who wasn't in the slightest bit criminal. On his first day on
remand a screw broke his nose for spitting, although when he
served the jail term at Long Lartin he told us that he was treated
pretty well, because that's what happens to armed robbers inside.
Later he was moved to an open prison. The family rallied round
and we visited him whenever we could, but it hit our parents
very hard.

Apart from politics, Dave's other abiding passion was blues music.
He acquired loads of blues records during the time he worked
with Erskine Thompson at the legendary Diskery record shop in
Birmingham. Erskine later became a mover in UK black music
circles, managing Maxi Priest in London and working with the
likes of Sly and Robbie and the Wailing Souls in Jamaica, but his
interest in music reached far and wide. David had built up a very
solid collection, but unfortunately his girlfriend sold them while
he was inside. Suffice to say that David is such a blues nut he has
rebuilt the entire collection and has thousands of albums to this
day.

But traditional folk music ruled the roost in Speedwell Road,
and dominated the radiogram in the front room. We weren't
allowed to play any of our stuff until the old man was out of the
house. Once he was gone, we'd get our latest reggae purchases
out and put them on. Mom loved to hear them and would come
in and even dance with us and our friends.

Early on we'd listen to the Beatles, the Everlys and the Stones
– if Dad wasn't around – while Dave would be up in his tiny
attic bedroom which contained his single bed, a record player,
seabird skulls and skeletons and blues albums. Nothing else.

Compared with those of our peers, our parents had pretty liber-
ated views on issues like race, equality and sex. Mother worked
at the Brook Advisory Centre and we would dish out pessaries

and condoms to our schoolmates. By the time the two younger boys were thirteen or so our mom made sure we had condoms in our pockets.

Ali was beaten at school once by a teacher during a lesson on the reproductive organs. He put his hand up and asked, 'Sir? Does a rat have a clitoris?' The only answer he got was several 'Whaaacks!' across the head.

Although we never had sit-downs about the birds and the bees with our parents, Mom would leave copies of *Men Only* and *Forum* around the house when we reached puberty so that we were in no doubt as to the ins and outs of sex.

'Mom was totally open with us, no subject was taboo,' says Robin. 'I can't remember a single occasion when we were discouraged from talking about sex or any aspect of anatomy. Our upbringing was very open.'

Ali and Duncan were sexually active from a young age. Often Robin would be sat downstairs watching the telly and Ali or Duncan would come home with girls from their school. It would be: 'We're just going upstairs to do our homework,' and then the bedsprings would start creaking. Because Duncan was advanced for his age, he led the way, and Ali followed, even getting freebies after standing by the side of the bed watching! Robin would be sat there mortified, listening to the shenanigans going on upstairs, while Mom and Dad ignored it completely.

'I could never have got away with that myself, not because our parents were any less open with me and Dave, but the times were different,' says Robin. 'Ali was lucky enough to have come of age during the permissive 70s. By the time of my first shag – when I was sixteen – Ali was already at it, and he's four years younger! I guess the times they were a-changing. I never brought a girl back to the house until I'd left home.'

As the youngest, Ali had a pretty safe passage through junior school. 'I was there as well, four years older, so if he was ever threatened, he could just counter-attack with threats of his big brothers,' Robin says. 'We were always very tribal: if there was any trouble it'd be the four of us who'd sort it out. Our primary school wasn't too bad, although it was on the outskirts of Balsall Heath. Secondary school was a lot different though.'

For Robin this was George Dixon's Grammar, an all-boys institution in City Road, Edgbaston. It had a very repressive atmosphere with mortar-boards, fags, gowns and canings. Because Dave was also at George Dixon's, there was a lot of 'Campbell Major' and 'Campbell Minor'.

Girls were unattainable, either angels or monsters, things of great beauty but not to be touched. On one occasion the head boy of George Dixon's was seen in the city centre holding hands with the head girl from the local girls' grammar school. Both shamefaced adolescents were paraded on stage in front of the entire assembly and then, while she sat with her head bowed, the head boy had his stripes ripped from his blazer by the deputy headmaster, such was his disgrace.

'I can't recall a more unhappy time in my life. They were the most miserable five years,' says Robin now. 'Everyone at school thought I was a total lunatic because I was a fan of funny music made by black men while they were all into prog-rock or pop. I was a definite oddity there, but wasn't bullied or anything like that. Where we lived it was a different matter, because, as a multiracial area, it was considered normal to be into reggae.

'The only ray of sunshine at school was a pupil called Ben Morbey. I could relate to him, a nice kid with a good sense of humour who also liked reggae, though he was from a well-to-do family, proper grammar-school material living in a posh house in Edgbaston. Ben's dad worked in television and he was a kid with his ear to the ground, always looking great, wearing the right Tonik trousers. That's how you knew he was well-off; his uniform was immaculate, with a Barathea blazer, which was the dog's, especially with metal buttons. Mine was made from thick felt and I was forced to wear shorts for a term into the second year, by which time all the other kids had graduated to long trousers. Ninety per cent of the people I've ever punched were those who laughed at me in my shorts. Any kid that made a remark very quickly learnt that my shorts were invisible. I'd hold them by their hair and punch their faces until they cried. Not that I had fights, as such. Every person that I hit went down immediately. That was the only trouble I got into.

'One of the teachers tried to persuade me to take up boxing as an outlet for my aggression. I thought about it for a few seconds but didn't want my face mashed up. For the same reason I wouldn't join in with the rugby. I didn't want a broken nose and cauliflower ears, but maybe that was where my lifelong love of watching boxing started.'

Rather than following the older brothers and attending George Dixon's, both Ali and Duncan underwent their secondary education at Moseley School of Art. 'Our parents weren't about to make the same mistake again,' says Robin. 'George Dixon's fucked up both Dave and me. We had always wanted to go to Moseley ourselves, but, apparently, the school was then run by a headmaster who some people thought was dreadful and our parents weren't prepared to send us there. By the time Ali and Duncan reached eleven, a new head had been appointed, which is why they went.'

Moseley School of Art wasn't an art college, as has sometimes mistakenly been reported, but a secondary modern with an art discipline. It was autonomous from the rest of the school system, the last of its kind in the country. Later it was amalgamated with Mount Pleasant School up the road and became the art annexe.

'It was a great little place, mainly because it only had 350 pupils in the entire school, as opposed to 350 per class at Mount Pleasant,' says Ali.

Ali admits that, by the time he went to secondary school, he had become an absolute terror, with more than a penchant for trouble and violence towards other pupils. All the working-class kids in the area were dressed in Oxford bags, Royals shoes, penny

collars and Barathea blazers, but, being the youngest, Ali was made
to wear brothers' hand-me-downs and a particularly humiliating
pair of orange Army boots.

'It turned me into a horrible child, as simple as that,' says Ali.
'Seriously, the effect of having to wear Duncan's clothes – and
him being twice my height – really pissed me off. I became a
bully because I was so resentful, a nasty kid. The irony is that I
actually liked school but I was so disruptive I wasn't allowed in
most of the lessons.'

One time Ali was caught persuading girls to feel his dick during
Miss Wills's textiles class, and on another occasion he hurled a
chair through a window. 'Once, when we had each dissected a
rat – and I don't know whether it had a clitoris or not – I threw
a piece which hit a student teacher in the face. I was suspended
for that and also for swearing at another teacher after a scuffle
when he ripped my shirt. I got a few slaps from Dad cause of
that one.'

With canings a regular occurrence, Ali mourns the fact that
the attitude of the teachers killed off his burgeoning fascination
for art.

'Any interest I had was knocked out of me,' he says. 'I wanted
to paint in oils and watercolours, draw still lifes, sculpture in clay.
At Moseley it was all: "Make this out of four bottle tops and a
hairbrush", that stuff. I just wasn't interested. It's not that I don't
like modern art – I think some of the stuff Damien Hirst has
done is brilliant and I like Warhol and the other pop artists. But
at that age I wanted to learn a traditional approach.'

Sometimes, even now, we get worked up about the ludicrous
folk clothing we were forced to wear as kids. Dad believes fashion
to be irrelevant, shallow and silly and he did everything he could
to discourage us from being interested in clothes, returning from
trips abroad with horrible hats and other ethnic stuff he would
force upon us. 'He'd come back from Denmark, or wherever, with
these stupid woollen hats which didn't go down at all well in

Balsall Heath,' says Ali. 'Unlike us, Duncan would wear lederhosen to the youth club. He was tall, so all you'd see were these long legs. We'd go: "You're fourteen Duncan and you've got a purple penny-collared shirt, fine! But why are you wearing those?" But he was just like our dad, believing that fashion was "stupid".'

So clothes were one of the things which we targeted when we went on the nick. By his early teens Robin had established quite a business for himself at school, as part of a gang which stole to order during the lunch hour and on the way home: Parker pens, cartridges, paint-brushes and geometry sets, which, if memory serves, were ten bob apiece to the other kids at school. We also stole racks and racks of cigarettes from the local Macfisheries supermarket by turning the security mirror the other way, and pillaged the department store Rackhams for records, Levi's and Wranglers. By the time Robin left school, he was making £15 a week; his first wage packet, at Harrison's Drapes, was just £8 a week, so it was quite a racket.

'I was caught a couple of times but wearing the George Dixon's blazer did have its benefits; going there was like going to Eton,' says Robin. 'If we were asked to empty our pockets by the security guards we'd turn it on: "What are you saying? This is dreadful. Ring my daddy, he's a High Court judge, he'll sort this out." One time when I was stopped, my blazer pockets were stuffed with Action Man bits and pieces for Ali, because he was obsessed with Action Man. Luckily I was wearing my overcoat so when I opened the blazer underneath there was nothing to see. I waddled out, absolutely loaded up.'

Once Mom found a carton of two hundred fags in Robin's room but she never questioned where it came from; parents want to believe the best, don't they? She was more upset by the fact that Robin was smoking in such quantities. He told her they were cheaper to buy in bulk and she took them off him, probably because she didn't have any herself! Anyway, he nicked them back over time.

More than clothes, Ali craved Action Man, forbidden in our house because it promoted militarism, so by the age of eleven he was also stalking Rackhams and Woolworth's. Ali and Duncan would offer to do Mom's shopping and then pocket the money they were given, stealing every item she wanted from Safeway and exiting through the back door. To our mom we were little angels, helping out with the household tasks. You tell her the truth now and she refuses to believe it. She had no idea and nor did the old man, because, even if he wasn't on the road while we were getting up to all sorts, musicians are fairly nocturnal creatures and we wouldn't see him much during the day. Ali would leave his contraband at Norman Hassan's house in Balsall Heath, where things were a lot easier, at least from that point of view.

Norman and Ali first met when they were both ten, little kids running around Balsall Heath. Looking back now it must have been very sad for Norman. His dad was from a pretty wealthy background in the Yemen, having been the owner of the main water well in his district. Then Norman's dad came over here and married his mom, who was Welsh, but went back to the Yemen when Norman and his sister Maria were just kids.

Their house had been very grand, but his mom was left destitute. She'd let all Norman's pals in the area drink, smoke and go out all night on adventures, nicking things and running riot.

'I met Norman when I started going to the Shell Youth Club, which was first in Balsall Heath and then moved to Moseley,' recalls Robin. 'There was a room there which played nothing but reggae. I started going when I was about fourteen, and introduced Ali and his gang to it. Norman was a roly-poly kid, because he'd had a kidney condition and was on steroids.'

Norman's mom was lovely, a bit of a Fagin character. 'She'd take us out to the shops and we'd thieve for her: make-up, food, brandy, whatever she wanted,' says Ali. 'Then Norman and I were caught stealing and I was barred from seeing him for a while. I remember his mom came to our house and told our parents what a terrible shock it had all been. She said she would never let Norman get up to that sort thing, when in fact she was the organiser! She's dead now, God rest her soul.'

Our parents divorced in the mid-70s. They'd had a pretty up-and-down relationship for many years. Mom was the long-suffering wife of a performing artist who was always on the road. We're not going to go into details here but it got to the point where she'd just had enough of the drinking and philandering. There was all sorts of stuff going on; he was having affairs which Mom would find out about.

At one stage, in the 60s, Dad even moved in with a girlfriend for a while. She only lived about half a mile up Speedwell Road, but eventually he came home. For a period Dad went away to take a degree as a mature student at Warwick University but came back home again.

During the final seven years of their marriage Mom wanted him to go but he just wouldn't leave. Ali recalls the occasion when Dad announced, 'Your mother's told me that she's not coming back until I leave. So please excuse me while I go and pack.'

Then he visited Robin. 'By that time I had my own flat and he came round to see me, asking where Mom was,' says Robin. 'I remember being really cold towards him; he was upset but I thought that he deserved it. He tried to tell me his personal problems but I didn't want to hear about them. I felt badly about that. Then, when I was about twenty-two, their divorce came through but it really didn't seem to be a big deal because by then they'd separated so many times.'

4

Reggae in your Jeggae

When we were kids, all of us brothers talked about forming our own group together, a close-harmony type of thing which we practised in our front room when the old man was out. If it had all worked out we were going to be Birmingham's version of the Jacksons. Ali was always our Michael, out front performing as the lead singer while the rest of us provided the backing vocals and harmonies.

The first time we sang together in front of family and friends was at a Hogmanay gathering in 1974 at our grandad's house in Spark Hill. Robin, Duncan and Ali rehearsed Stevie Wonder's song 'Village Ghettoland' in three-part harmony and delivered it well. Everyone clapped, seeming to enjoy it. Then, as the applause subsided, Grandad said in his strong Scottish brogue, 'What beautiful voices lads; it's a shame you're singing such shite!' But we didn't care. By then we were both strongly in the grip of reggae and soul. Unlike the rest of the family, we weren't even vaguely interested in folk, although growing up in an atmosphere where everybody would burst into song at the drop of a hat made it easier for us to start singing the music we liked. While Duncan was bang into folk he had pretty eclectic tastes and also harboured a love for reggae and soul, and the only other exception to the folk fervour was our cousin Angus, Lorna's son. He got into really out-there stuff, jazz-rock fusion. His group even performed at Gran and Grandad's golden wedding party, though there were lots of complaints about the volume! In the 90s Angus formed B15 Project, who recorded for Ali's label, Orocabessa, and later scored a Number 2 hit with the song 'Girls Like Us' with Chrissy D and Lady G.

But we're getting ahead of ourselves. Back in the mid-60s at the age of twelve, Robin started really getting into Jamaican music, and Ali didn't need any persuading by the insistent rhythms.

We frequented shops like Don Christie's on Ladypool Road, which was *the* place to learn about our favourite music. The shop would pump out reggae records non-stop all day. You wouldn't know one track from another, so the only way to get hold of them was to say: 'I'll have that one,' while a single was still spinning, or else they would go straight onto the next one and you'd lose the chance to grab it.

Sometimes, if you went in looking for a specific tune, Don might play that for you, although Robin was actually given his first reggae record by a friend who knew he was a fan. 'This was back in 1966,' reminisces Robin. 'It was an EP of various Jamaican number ones by Millie & Her Boyfriends. She'd already had a hit with 'My Boy Lollipop' and on this EP she sang duets with different male singers, people like Jackie Edwards.'

Don also had a shop in the Rag Market, which was a bit less threatening for little white kids, so when we were younger we'd go see him there. Our fascination with reggae also had something to do with our hormones. It was the sexiest sound around. When we were budding teenagers, going into a blues – as the house parties were called – and hearing that bass-line throb in a pitch-dark environment was so alluring.

We always assumed they were called blues as a contraction of 'rhythm and blues parties' though we've also heard that they were named after the first sound systems, which were invariably those old German Blaupunkt ('blue point') radiograms you saw everywhere in the 50s and 60s. You could really crank them up high because the speakers were so good.

At the earliest blues in the 50s, when the first wave of Caribbean immigrants were settling into Britain, you would hear calypso, jazz and New Orleans rock and roll. By the time Robin bowled along there was still a smattering of that stuff played by the older dudes, but there would also be ska and rocksteady which both kicked in during the mid-60s, as well as reggae, as it started to be called in the latter part of that decade.

'I went to my first blues around the age of twelve, with a mate of mine,' says Robin. 'We'd heard about them from some older kids and found out this particular one was being held in Balsall Heath. It was all planned beforehand. My mate waited outside my house while I pretended to go to bed and then crept out of the kitchen window, down the sloping roof, into the garden, and met up with him. We made our way to this house and found ourselves in this darkened room with a red bulb, full of grown-ups. Apart from us everyone else was black and although at first it was strange and scary, they were cool and let us just soak it all in. This was before reggae had really started to happen, so they were listening to ska and bluebeat, and tunes like "Blueberry Hill" by Fats Domino, New Orleans boogie-woogie.'

To go to a blues or a late club and dance with a girl to reggae was almost like having sex. The way we danced meant that every inch of you would be touching your partner.

It was also important that we first got our first real exposure to reggae at blues, because that's where the bass line really gets hold of you. People who haven't heard reggae at one of those things don't fully understand it. A tune starts with killer treble and then, when they kick the bass in, the whole building starts to shake and you either feel nauseous or really happy. Long before raves, going to a blues was like an assault on your senses. Techno raves are really just white man's blues; there you get off your face and the bass drives through you. There's no difference to the experience.

We were surrounded by this infectious music, so you couldn't help but fall in love with it. It's too simplistic to say that we got into reggae as a form of rebellion against the old man. We just loved it for what it was. Whenever reggae broke into the charts we were proud, no matter how pop the song was.

Even Judge Dread and his dirty ditties made us pleased that our music was being represented. We were really excited when Desmond Dekker was on *Top of the Pops* doing 'Israelites', or Ken Boothe in his flares singing 'Everything I Own'. Robin was a suedehead in all the gear – Crombie, Toniks, button-down check shirt, brogues – with singles like 'Monkey Spanner' by Dave and Ansil Collins and 'Liquidator' by Harry J. All Stars.

When Robin wasn't around, Ali would 'borrow' his singles, starting at the age of ten. 'Me and Duncan would take them to the local youth club and hold dances, with all the kids jumping up and down to this great music,' says Ali. 'Because he recognised I was just as into the music as him, I became Robin's little mascot and started following him to blues. I was already drinking and smoking at that age. Our parents would have gone mad if they'd found out, so I would visit Norman, ostensibly to stay the night. Then we would imitate what Robin had done a few years earlier: pretend to go to bed and sneak out the window and join him.'

Within a few years a radical new version of reggae arrived on these shores: Dub. A wicked hybrid of sound, filled not only with danceable rhythms but also spacey echoes, dub reflected perfectly what goes on inside your head when you're toking on a spliff, dancing tight with a girl and soaking up the atmosphere of a blues.

Up until that point reggae production had been pretty basic, but dub was created by inspired sound-system operators and producers like King Tubby and Lee 'Scratch' Perry utilising all manner of sound techniques and studio wizardry at their disposal.

Dub got its name from the heavy-duty acetates from which vinyl records were cut. The 'dub plates' were spun at all-night dances when Tubby and the rival sound systems literally mixed and fucked with the sound as it bled through the giant speakers.

By the mid-70s Bob Marley was breaking through in England as the first real reggae star, having been marketed like a rock act with proper tours and promotion by Chris Blackwell at Island Records. Blackwell would later say that our own music had 'no commercial value', but that's for later in the story.

We both went to see Marley and the Wailers just as he was crossing over in 1975 at the Birmingham Odeon, one of the best gigs ever. The great album *Live at the Lyceum* came from a date recorded in London just a couple of days later.

Seeing Marley live was such an inspiration. With the Wailers and his backing vocalists, the I–Threes, the show was a tour de force and affirmation that reggae wasn't a minority interest but had the potential to appeal to everybody, black and white. 'Going to that gig was probably the single event which made us want to form a reggae band,' says Robin. 'We just didn't know how.' As Marley led the way for reggae, dub was the sound of the street and in the clubs and blues: big, booming bass, phased melodies swooping in and out and delayed, distorted vocals, repeated and made supersonic by the wired production techniques.

Blues were also the place where we first encountered weed. 'It took me a year or so to pluck up courage and accept the offer of a joint,' says Robin. 'If one was being passed around when I started going, I'd say, "No, you're alright," but when I was about thirteen I took a couple of puffs and passed it back. It hit me hard but I had a great time, just stood there, eyes glazed, absorbing it all. The sensation was beautiful, and it was the final part of the jigsaw for properly experiencing a blues; you had the bass shaking your ribcage, the treble stinging your eyes, the rhythms moving your body and the weed making your brain float and spin. As a teenager I never bought draw though. I'd pay £1 for single joints. Even then I'd share it with me mates, maybe even ten of us; I never had a joint to myself until I was in my thirties.'

Ali, who had been smoking fags and drinking from the age of eight, also started smoking draw at thirteen or so. 'I knew the smell long before I tried it,' he says. 'Mention a blues to me and it evokes the smell of the seeds popping as the spliffs were smoked. These were the days before *sensimilla* [Spanish for seedless female plant]. Norman and I weren't offered any weed at the blues we went to, probably because they thought we were too young, so the first draw I had was when I was thirteen, from a kid in the sixth form who was known for being a dope smoker.'

By steeping ourselves in reggae it was inevitable that we would be drawn to weed, which is such an integral part of the reggae experience.

Our draw smoking never became an issue with our parents. Though we weren't allowed to smoke at home, the old man had been part of the 60s folk scene, and his fiddle player, Dave Swarbrick, smoked like a chimney. 'I know Dad and Mom had a smoke of pot at parties and gatherings back then,' says Robin. 'Later on in our lives, if there was draw around us, they'd have a smoke with us.'

When the family moved away from Balsall Heath we soon realised how much reggae was part of our lives, simply because it wasn't played that much in other neighbourhoods. We had a new home in the slightly nicer area of King's Heath, a different world musically. Nobody our age seemed to know or care about reggae there, so we spent every waking hour going back to where we came from, getting a bus over on Friday night and not coming back home until last thing on Sunday evening, staying up all night or at friends' houses, hanging out in cafés and blues.

Our formative experiences at the blues and in Don Christie's were the inspiration for *Labour Of Love* much later on in our lives. We knew all of those tracks as smash hits in our area, they're the songs we grew up with: 'Red Red Wine' by Tony Tribe, 'Cherry Oh Baby' by Eric Donaldson. We only found out that Neil Diamond owned the publishing rights to 'Red, Red Wine' when we cleared them for our version. We always thought it was a reggae song just like all the others, and in fact if you listen to Tony Tribe's it's obviously a cover of the version by Jimmy James & the Vagabonds, not Neil Diamond's. Nobody outside Balsall Heath really knew that much about those tracks; to us it was as though they were all new songs.

Ali's first reggae record was 'Reggae in your Jeggae' by Dandy, who later made his name as Dandy Livingstone and had a pop hit with 'Suzanne Beware of the Devil'. 'Reggae in your Jeggae' – one of the rash of releases inspired by what is thought to be the first reggae record, 'Do the Reggay' by the Maytals – was given to Ali by our cousin Debbie, who was then a bit of a hippy. She gave it to Ali with one of those portable record players for singles. For a long time it was the only record played on that portable, again and again and again.

At one time we both had pretty comprehensive collections covering everything from ska to dancehall, from Lover's Rock to ragga, but these days they have been much reduced. Robin lost hundreds of rare albums and singles through theft in the 70s, while Ali's collection was amalgamated with that of his roadie and best mate Pops, who was bang into Lover's Rock. During one tour Pops's now ex girlfriend flogged the lot while they were away from home. Unforgivable!

For many years our father was absolutely disgusted with our obsession with reggae. As a contemporary folk musician he was into traditional music, hands cupped to the ear in time-honoured fashion, the whole thing, and pretty narrow-minded. He never gave reggae music a chance, just wasn't prepared to understand it at all. Then in the late 70s Dad suddenly experienced an overnight conversion, to Bob Marley if not to reggae as a whole. A very good friend of his, the folk singer Bob Davenport, really rates Marley and sings his songs very well in a traditional vein. He even does 'Get Up, Stand Up', an incredible version. It still gives us both goose-pimples when we hear him sing it.

One time the old man was talking about this shit that the lads were into and Bob Davenport said to him, 'Hang on Ian, have you ever listened to Marley? He's a genius!'

Because they'd been friends for twenty years and Bob is a trusted traditionalist, Dad finally caved in. Since then he has grudgingly admitted, 'Marley is OK.'

5

The Right Not to Work

There are so many reasons why we formed the band; with hind-sight it seems like it was fated. Maybe it was. But it certainly didn't happen overnight. Robin was invited to leave George Dixon's Grammar a year early, at the age of fifteen in the summer of 1969, so wasn't allowed to take his GCEs. He became an apprentice toolmaker at Harrison's Drapes, the factory in Birmingham which produced curtain rails.

'For the first few years I was doing very well, getting distinctions and credits,' he says. 'After a while, my wages improved from the starting point of £8.12s. 7d. a week and at one time I was the highest-paid apprentice in the Midlands.'

But the job itself was far from stimulating and all his mates were having a hell of a time earning top whack with their jobs on building sites. At the beginning of 1972, with eight months left of his apprenticeship, Robin announced he was leaving.

Our dad was furious. He brought home friends and family members such as our grandad to help dissuade Robin from his course of action. 'They were all craftsmen, people who tried to convince me not to throw my trade away,' says Robin. 'It was a pretty stupid move, but I was a typical eighteen-year-old and couldn't take it any more. I was on £15 a week and my mates on the sites were on £40 a week, so I joined them.'

The career change exacerbated tensions at home. Dad wouldn't let up and Robin wasn't prepared to discuss it. The rowing got to such a pitch that it was decided Robin should move to a house in nearby Stirchley shared by our brother David and a couple of his friends, students at Bournville College.

'There was a spare room — it was my mom's idea because it was clear that me and my dad couldn't live under the same roof. But she could still keep an eye on me at my brother's place.'

It was a brilliant idea, and after a few months the rest of them moved out, as the regularly shifting cast of student tenants drifted in and out of there. Among the characters who lived in the house for a while was this guy John Brown, who performed blues songs in local folk clubs. 'I had no ambition to be in a band at that stage,' says Robin. 'I had the six chords I'd been taught by my uncle, Dad's guitar player Brian Clark, when I was much younger, and John Brown showed me a few more. He was into Leadbelly and blues and folk stuff, and showed me how to pick. I got an acoustic guitar and used to mess around, but wasn't at all serious.'

By this time Robin had got together with his future wife, Sally Barnes, and was a bit of a face-about-town as a hardcore clubber. 'I'd been to junior school with Sally — she used to chase me around the playground when I was ten or eleven,' says Robin. 'I hadn't seen her for years, but we met again at a dance in Selly Oak when I was seventeen. She was absolutely transformed; she had been a bit overweight as a kid, but by the time we met again she was very attractive, similar to Paula Wilcox, the 70s sitcoms actress.

'I was at the bar with my mate Mel and spotted her. Before I could make a move she came over and said, "Don't I know you?" I found out subsequently that she didn't actually remember me;

it was just a chat-up line. We started seeing each other and were together until I left to join the band.'

Sometimes Ali would meet up with the young couple. 'I used to go over and see Robin a lot. One of the attractions was that Sally had the Jackson Five album *Maybe Tomorrow*,' recalls Ali. 'They were great to me, and took me along when they went to see the Jackson Five at the Birmingham Odeon in 1974.'

We had the best tickets in the house, and the queue seemed to go on for ever. Instead of joining it at the back we said to each other, 'If anybody tries to stop you, just ignore them,' and walked straight in to our seats, unchallenged.

By this time Robin had long been heading for the reggae rooms of the larger clubs, dancing to all the stuff which ended up on *Labour of Love*. 'You had to seek reggae out in those days,' he says. 'It could be found if you looked hard enough, usually in the sweaty pit of a basement, or stuck away in a cramped attic. Because I hung out at reggae shops like Don Christie's and the blues, I'd find out which club nights played the music.

'Between the ages of fifteen and twenty I guess I thought of myself as a bit of a hard man, always getting into scrapes,' says Robin. 'Even in my early twenties I would do really stupid things like pinching a Cortina 1600E because I was drunk and wanted to get home.

'Once I was fined £15 for disorderly conduct for singing "Hey screw don't bother me" along with my mates at some coppers one night. We were pointing at them and laughing, and thought they had walked off. When we got to our bus stop, five pandas swooped in and nicked the lot of us, especially after my pal Skinhead Mick – a right little monster who'd been inside loads of times – kicked off with a few of the cadets. They beat the shit out of him.

'But music was my abiding passion. I would be off four or five nights a week at reggae places like the Nocturne, the top room at the Locarno Ballroom, which was rough as arseholes. That was one of the places in the city centre where all the black kids went. Later I was always at the Futrell brothers' clubs in town: Barbarella's, the Cedar, Rebecca's. That's where I saw Johnny Nash, the Drifters and Rufus, Chaka Khan's band and many more.'

Around about that time Ali made an abrupt exit from Moseley School of Art, where his unruly behaviour had made him a marked pupil among the teaching staff.

'I was suspended,' he says. 'There had been an altercation with a teacher where I told him to fuck off after he ripped my shirt in the classroom. He sent me to the headmaster's office, where I was ordered to bend over the desk and take the cane. I was sixteen by then and wasn't going to have it so I was invited to leave. I decided to accept.'

Ali was allowed to take O levels in English Literature and English Language, Art, Geography and History, and achieved respectable grades in all subjects. 'I had no interest in anything but music when I left school,' says Ali, 'so I couldn't care less about work. I did some stints as a labourer and even worked as an industrial cleaner. Eventually I was on the dole for three-and-a-half years, such a long time. They made me sign on every day.'

In 1976, just as Ali was embarking on his protracted stint of unemployment, fate took a violent twist on the night of his seventeenth birthday, 15 February, when he went out for a drink with Robin's best mate Melvin and Earl Falconer, a friend who had also gone to Moseley School of Art.

'We were drinking in the Red Lion,' says Ali. 'I was running up my mouth at the bar and somebody evidently didn't like what they heard, because a bit later, while we were out in the corridor, this couple were arguing over whether she should leave. She told him that her dad was waiting outside and I said something like: "Oh! Overbearing father, eh?"'

'He was straight onto me: "You what? You what? Think you're fucking hard, do you?"'

'I said: "No. I think I'm fucking drunk," and then I was smacked full in the face with one of those heavy old pint mugs. The fight spilled outside, Earl was defending me from him and his mates, as I staggered around holding my face and then grabbed a branch from a tree and started swinging it about.

'When the fighting finally stopped I realised that I couldn't open my left eye. They took me off to Birmingham Eye Hospital and Earl stayed with me while Mel went back to our house.'

Robin recalls the night clearly. 'Mel told us what had happened,' he says. 'It's the only time I have ever seen Mom truly, truly beside herself. She was so scared.'

But luck was on Ali's side. Birmingham Eye Hospital had been visited that day by top consultant and specialist surgeon Sir Vernon Smith, who was still on the premises after having given a lecture.

'He saved my eye by performing a lens transplant,' says Ali. 'At the time it wasn't the practice to give transplants to patients under thirty-five years old.'

Ali had ninety sutures on the left side of his face and to his eye. It is a testament to Smith's skill that he is virtually unmarked. 'He was brilliant,' says Ali. 'But for him, I really do believe I'd be blind with a face full of bootlaces!'

Ali spent a month in hospital, and later our brother Dave filed a claim for compensation for criminal injuries on Ali's behalf, as he was working as a legal executive at the time.

By the early summer of 1976 Ali was fully recovered, though the vision in his left eye has never been the same since. He decided to get away from Brum and went off with Duncan to work the summer season at Butlin's in Barry Island, South Wales.

However – unlike many other public figures who served their turn toiling away at holiday camps – Ali was never an entertainer at Butlin's. You can't really see him in a red coat, can you?

'Our mom had bought us a smart suit each, and when we went along to be interviewed they put us in the queue for the admin department and we both became cashiers,' says Ali. 'That's where I was given The Gift: the key to the meters in the self-catering chalets! One of my tasks every Saturday was to empty the meters once the residents had moved out. It really was a gift placed straight into my hands.

'I'd rifle the meters and when the new people arrived I'd be there, offering change, so my ill-gotten gains were converted into notes. I did the whole season and was probably the richest seventeen-year-old in Britain at the time.'

Bingo was a different matter. Because you had to make everything tally, Duncan and Ali were provided with less opportunities to fatten their wallets, though calling out the numbers helped exercise their vocal talents.

At the end of the season Ali returned home and Robin was running the bar at the Jug. 'I was twenty-one, which was ridiculously young to be doing that job in those days,' says Robin. 'I also had the keys! In some ways we really have led a charmed life!'

With the folk boom well and truly over, the Jug now occupied the basement of what later became Albert's Wine Bar in Albert Street and had themed weekly clubs: Rock Night with Nimrod, a Jazz Sunday and our dad's folk club every Thursday.

We decided to start the reggae night which was held on Fridays. 'Dad and Lorna had gone off on tour,' says Ali. 'They didn't know anything about it. We just came up with the plan to take over the Friday night spot and by the time they got back it was chocker, so they let us carry on.'

At the time there weren't that many reggae bands in Britain. In Brum, reggae had been restricted to places like the Top Rank and the Rainbow Suites, off the Smallbrook Ring Road.

But we packed them in. The Jug saw the first gig in Birmingham by pioneering Brit-reggae artists Matumbi. Steel Pulse would come over from Handsworth and play there, and we'd have the local sound systems: Studio One, Count Spaceman Sound and Duke Alloy, whose DJs included Astro, later to join UB40.

'We ran the bar,' says Robin. 'The booker of the night would always try and knock the bands for their performance fee, foisting them off on us with an excuse that we'd look after them. After Matumbi played they all came over asking for their £200. We pointed them in his direction and he offered them £50!'

When Lorna and Dad came back, Ali had been working at the Jug for six or seven weeks. As usual it was the full-on family affair with all the Campbells involved in one way or another. 'Lorna told me that I wasn't old enough to be working behind the bar, and ordered me to help my granny on the door,' says Ali. 'I told her that I wasn't there to do anybody any favours, but to help Rob at the bar. She stormed off and then Dad appeared, just before he was due to go on stage. He said, "I'll tell you what, you can do me a favour." Then he nutted me!'

Robin adds: 'I didn't see it happen, but next thing Dad was up on stage singing, and this huge lump started to appear on his own head. As soon as Ali told me what had happened, I locked the till and closed the bar. We were out of there. The old man came running across apologising profusely. I told him, "Don't apologise to me – it's him you just butted in the face!" Eventually he talked us into reopening the bar.'

Our involvement with the reggae nights was over soon afterwards. We still didn't have much of an idea about how to form a band beyond just talking about it. None of us had any money, and the only one of us who could play an instrument was Robin, who decided he needed a regular wage again and took a job at the British Leyland plant. 'I joined as an operator and ended up as a setter/operator, an easy job for which I was overqualified,' he says. 'It was a good solid wage and I didn't fancy going back on the buildings. At least I realised by then how stupid I'd been to have taken that up.'

Robin and Sally moved into a flat in a house in Longbridge rented by our brother David, who was on his extended holiday at Her Majesty's Pleasure. They had married in 1976 at a registry office

An early picture of our mom's mom and dad, Jack and Amy Weaver.

Our paternal grandparents Betty and Dave Campbell.

The brothers together at Nan and Granddad Weaver's house in Great Barr, early 60s. From left: Robin, Ali, Dave and Duncan.

Ali gives it some biker attitude, early 60s.

Ali as pageboy. 'Little did they know I was off my head on shandy.'

Ali all smiles amid the purple heather, Bardsey Island, early 60s.

Campbells sing up in support of the miners, 1984.
From left: Neil Cox, Lorna, Grandma, Dad, Grandad and Aidan Ford.

Family gathering, 1982: From left: Dad, behind him cousin Angus, Lorna, Grandad,
Duncan, Dave, us two, Grandma, Mom.

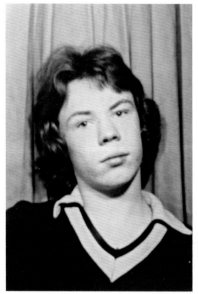

Ali in a photo booth, 1975.

Ali in 1981 with Ali Jnr on his lap.

At home, 1985. From left: Duncan, Ali, Mom, Robin, Dave.

Jimmy and Ali, mid 80s.

Poster for one of the series of gigs we did in London in the summer of 1979.

Our first album sleeve. A copy of the Unemployment Benefit Form 40, so familiar to all of us.

Robin on Ali: 'These days I've got my brother back, full of enthusiasm and energy. He's doing the best work of his career.'

Ali on Robin: 'He's the one soundchecking his guitar all through the day and then all through the gig, even though he has a roadie to do all that.'

Early 80s passport photographs.

Robin and Norman in a thoughtful mood at an early recording session.

in Solihull, succumbing to pressure from Sally's parents about making an honest woman of her. But Robin was already experiencing misgivings about the long-term future of the relationship.

'I was going through a serious transitional phase in my life; I was holding down this regular job by working at British Leyland but knew that Sally and I weren't really suited,' says Robin. 'It was all too scary; I could see myself old and grey in the same job and trapped in a loveless marriage.

'My best man was our brother Duncan, who knew I was only doing it for her and her family. Just before we entered the registry office, Duncan looked me in the eye and said, "It's not too late. We can go now. You don't have to do this." But I had to go through with it. They were all waiting inside.

'The registrar gave me the most lethal look when he saw the grin on my face, because I couldn't take it seriously. That set Duncan off and soon I had Ali and all these other twats laughing openly during the ceremony.'

Robin was dressed very much in the style of the times: 'I wore an immaculate navy pinstripe suit. The jacket had a 24-inch vent at the back and four-and-a-half inch lapels while the trousers were waisted to fuck with 34-inch bottoms. In the wedding photographs you can't see the platform shoes I've got on! If you took little steps you looked like a Dalek when you walked, as though you were hovering just above the ground! For my best mate Mel's wedding the following year I had the trousers reduced to a 30-inch bottom, or else they would have looked stupid. . .'

At Leyland, Robin made gears for the Maxi 1850, setting a multi-cast lathe, using gauges and measurements. 'The mind-numbing aspect was having to make a certain amount of these every shift,' he says. 'But the time-and-motion studies which gave you the target meant that, if you knew what you were doing, you could reach your quota in a few hours. Then you could take a kip or do a crossword.

'When I worked nights I would leave the machinery running

and play chess with my mates for the whole shift. That's how hard the work was: after six months on nights I became very good at chess.'

During that stint Robin would finish every Friday morning and not have to start work again until Monday night. 'I'd be gone for the weekend,' says Robin. 'Snooker, clubbing it, blues, it was nothing for me to disappear for several nights. Sally was an absolute angel about it. She would never give me any grief. She had also come to realise we were poles apart.'

Meanwhile Ali had moved out of our family home and lived in various places around Moseley. One of the Suburban Studs – a local punk band who had a reputation for being very loud – lived in a flat above one of Ali's, and even he complained about the noise!

'The circle I moved in got into selling dope,' says Ali. 'None of us on the Moseley scene had money or jobs, so we'd sell at places like the Shoop, which was run by Mike Horseman, who later became the manager of the Beat. We'd also go to the grebo haunt, Bogarts. We'd pay £6 for an eighth of black or Red Leb a week and smoke a lot of it ourselves. We'd give the bikers a draw and then sell them boot polish wrapped in silver foil. You'd fuck off out of there as soon as the deals were done and before they found out!'

Ali and friends such as Norman, who by then was a carpet fitter, constantly dreamt of becoming part of a famous band and achieving their ultimate goal: acquiring an ounce of hash and not allowing anybody to leave until the lot had been smoked. 'These days we all smoke at least an ounce each a week!' he exclaims.

By the start of 1978, after two years on the dole, Ali was having a horrible time. 'There I was living with Jimmy, and sometimes Earl as well, each of us on £7.90 a week. We were on our own and having to fend for ourselves. We were basically thieves, although we mainly stole food.

'We couldn't get jobs anyway, so Jimmy, Earl and I started our own local version of the Claimants' Union in Balsall Heath with our friend Jimmy Lynn, even going to the extent of making ourselves identity cards. If you've ever been on the dole you'll know what a merry dance they lead you, so we formed this local branch to help people like elderly Nigerian ladies claim the money to which they were rightfully entitled.'

A lot of our conversations started to centre on this idea of forming a band. But the idea of a mixed-race reggae band had never been tried before, and we just didn't know how to go about it. Punk had taken over and there seemed no place for the likes of us.

At the time, with the late 70s unemployment crisis looming, one of the popular slogans was 'The Right To Work', but Ali and his friends had another idea: 'We thought that was pointless,' he says. 'We started to get into the idea of the right *not* to work. Maybe, we thought, that would open our options up a little.'

6

Unemployment Benefit Form 40

It seemed to us in the summer of 1978 that everyone we knew was forming a band, particularly in Moseley where there was a group occupying every other house.

The DIY punk attitude ruled: anyone could be in a band, you didn't actually have to be able to play an instrument proficiently. In some ways, although none of us ever really liked punk music – apart from Brian – the formation of UB40 was fuelled by that punk ethic.

That year, Ali in particular was always going on about it. Ever since we were kids we'd held out a hope that we'd become musicians and now he kept on saying that the time was right.

Dad always had his own way of dealing with the music business and instilled in us the drive to do things our way. We knew from the get-go that we wanted the group to be multicultural and multi-instrumental and that all decisions and music-making would be democratic. Although this has often led us into a world of nightmares and compromise, we still operate on that basis. After all, we have all known each other for ever. Jimmy, Earl and Brian Travers were all with Ali at Moseley School of Art, while Mickey

Virtue and Astro – who would both join after the first few gigs – went to Golden Hillock comprehensive together. Norman, of course, had (not) been at Mount Pleasant and was one of our closest mates since him and Ali were in short trousers.

People ask whether it has been difficult being brothers and working so closely in the same band. But the fact is we treat each other just as we treat every other UB40 member. We all have an equal say in what happens, so we're all brothers.

We've always fought like cats and dogs but the thing that has made UB40 since day one is that it's a total compromise; each person carries the same weight in arguments and decision-making. Nobody likes to compromise but we all have to, which can be very frustrating for us individually but not for the group as a whole. Maybe that's why it continues to work to this day. UB40 is essentially eight people compromising continuously.

From the very beginning we agreed that reggae was the natural choice of music to play. We didn't claim we discovered it, but we were always on a mission to promote it and in some ways we still are, twenty-five years later.

As we have said, most of the band weren't that enamoured of the punk movement. 'We all went to see the Clash play a huge Rock Against Racism rally in the East End in 1978,' says Ali. 'There were hundreds of thousands of kids jumping up and down in Victoria Park in Hackney. Instead of staying, we decided we'd have a go at the National Front, who had organised a march down Brick Lane that day. When we got there we were the only ones, the rest of the would-be protestors preferred to stay at the gig rather than actually do something to stop the fascists throwing bricks at ethnic minorities. We were hideously outnumbered by all these skinheads, dumbos and morons and eventually had to run for it.'

We'd always gone along to political demonstrations, so it wasn't as though we were bandwagon-jumpers when politics and music became so intertwined. We were at Lewisham in 1977 protesting over the NF march; at Red Lion Square years earlier when there was a massive fight with the police and student Kevin Gately was killed, and also at the Winson Green riots which were described at the time as the worst outbreak of civil disobedience since the Second World War.

Even when the Young National Front tried to set up in Digbeth we were there to kick ass. But we never wanted to ally ourselves to a single political movement, whether it was Rock Against Racism or Red Wedge. In our view they were all a bunch of self-righteous middle-class wankers perpetuating the myth that by demonstrating you're actually having an effect, when we knew that action speaks far louder than words.

In those days we were hanging out with all the other bands in Moseley and became the gang who did all the parties. Having knocked around together at school, the dole office was where we all met up again. The only ones with jobs were Robin and Brian. The rest of us had time on our hands and, before we even had any instruments, we decided to form a group.

With Robin's marriage to Sally drifting, a deciding factor came in the form of the offer of a foreman's job at the Leyland plant.

'I'd been there for a couple of years, and had done my six months on nights, all the things you're supposed to do,' says Robin. 'I went off on holiday that year, and, as I was leaving, they said, "There's a blue coat for you when you come back if you want it."

'I knew that if I took that blue coat I would be there for the rest of my life,' he says. 'So I bit the bullet and never went back, playing snooker to get some money in. I'd take a job for a few months and then just fuck off for the summer. Sally and I didn't have kids and weren't planning them, so I didn't have too many responsibilities. Then Sally got a job as a croupier in town and her lifestyle changed. She became a night person, so a lot of our time was spent apart. If I stayed in I was on my own, and if I was out and about I was with my mates or over in Moseley. I was moving in bohemian circles and she was four or five nights a week at the casino, so we never saw each other. Our lives completely diverged.'

Robin had spent time with Duncan, trying all sorts of hair-brained money-raising schemes, none of which were successful. 'We organised a Christmas Fair once, tried to run a bingo hall, with Dunc calling out Legs Eleven and the rest,' says Robin. 'I think I've had thirty different jobs in my time, some of which lasted a couple of hours. In those days you could literally walk into a job and if you didn't fancy it you'd be out of there. Once I went along to this factory and became a lathe turner. I arrived and this guy said, "Here's your lathe, and this is your post for the next seven hundred years. . ." I told him, "I've just got to get something from my car," and was gone. I was there for eight minutes, didn't even have a cup of tea!'

Then good fortune struck: Ali received £4,000 in compensation for the eye injury he sustained during the pub fight a couple of years earlier.

'One day the cheque just arrived in the post,' he says. 'It was a lot of money then and seemed like pennies from heaven, the very thing we needed, at exactly the right time. I decided to dedicate most of it to instruments so that we could form a band, though a lot of it was spent down the pub!'

Ali also lent Robin and Duncan a grand to help them realise their plans to get into the used-car business by buying and selling in the local papers.

'There was one problem: we were absolutely fucking useless,' says Robin.

'One of the first things we bought was a left-hand-drive GT6 which we couldn't get rid of. We were spectacularly poor at the car game, probably because we were playing snooker all the time.'

At first, Ali, Jimmy and Earl had one instrument, a violin-bodied Gibson Bass copy bought for Earl by his missus, Dawn. Soon they added a conga drum and a Stylophone and Jimmy dragged along the drum kit his dad had bought him when he was at school and into jazz-fusion, people like Billy Cobham and Chick Corea, really pretentious stuff. He had even played in a band which was part of the Bahai faith. It's rumoured that Jimmy had an Elton John album, though he'd probably claim it was his sister's.

'Jimmy's kit was crap, so we bought another from a junkie in Moseley village,' says Ali. 'We knew this geezer was in a bad way when we bartered him down from his £300 asking price to just £35. The drums were fire-damaged, so we peeled the skins off, glued Bacofoil on and varnished them. Then it looked like an amazing silver kit, and we flogged it for a few hundred quid – I think to the Beat – to buy ourselves a really decent set of drums.' With Ali's compensation we added some more equipment and 'acquired' the rest. Ali picked up a guitar from a party in Moseley. It was a right-handed Rapier 28 – no good for left-handed Ali, so Earl broke it in half and turned it into one suitable for him to play.

Then, in the late summer of 1978, Robin was coerced into attending a jam by Jimmy, Earl and Ali at Cannon Hill Arts Centre. 'I thought they were shocking,' grimaces Robin at the memory. 'Absolutely dreadful and certainly nothing I wanted to be involved in. I left them to it.'

Undeterred by Robin's criticism and their lack of musical skills, the trio decamped to the cellar underneath Brian's flat at 106 Trafalgar Road, Moseley. 'We broke into the cellar, rigged the electric, which was easy since Brian was an apprentice sparks, and got ourselves a little rehearsal studio,' says Ali. 'The landlord didn't know a thing about it.'

In the cellar the musicians worked diligently, rehearsing every day and joined by pals such as Norman on percussion. For the first few months there was a second percussionist, our friend Yomi Babayemi. Yomi was full of enthusiasm, a real ball of energy we knew from the Moseley scene. 'One of Yomi's things was to roll a really thin neat spliff, but the roach would take up most of it,' recalls Ali. 'We'd sit there watching him smoke it, and by the time it was passed around all that was left was cardboard.'

Brian was also contributing. He'd had a sax in his possession for some time, but never bothered to play it. He preferred to draw outlines around it to decorate walls and even seriously considered flattening it and hanging it as an art object. As soon as he saw that we were actually doing something about our ambitions he started to learn and mastered it pretty quickly.

'Brian's entry into music had been hanging outside punk clubs, offering to shift gear for the bands as they turned up for soundchecks,' says Robin. 'That way he'd get into the gig. He ended up a roadie for the Suburban Studs.'

Soon the trio and their friends had built up a limited set based on their own compositions, all of them instrumentals with Ali playing guitar, Earl on bass and Jimmy on drums. Among these very first UB40 songs were 'Mother Country', which later became 'My Way of Thinking', and the instrumental 'Bouncing Around', which was to be transformed in the mid-80s into our hit 'If It Happens Again'. There was a track called 'Broken Windows' (by Randy Newman), and 'Gibson Bass', named after that instrument bought for Earl by his missus. We also covered Bim Sherman's 'Lover's Leap' and Gregory Isaacs's 'Mr Know It All'.

'It was during our time rehearsing in the cellar that I had the first really strong weed of my life,' says Ali. 'This long-distance lorry driver we knew called Johnny Wragg had just got back from Nigeria. He dropped round with a bag of this serious green weed. That was my first time having an anxiety attack and the out-of-body experience. It was frightening, and brilliant and new, all at the same time. I didn't know what the hell had hit me. These days I smoke just to get an out-of-body experience'.

That day Robin recalls us two taking for ever to walk a few hundred yards down Trafalgar Road. 'It took us all day, we were so stoned and laughing our heads off, talking blancmange underwater at each other,' he says. 'There were two old dears passing by who looked really scared; we were desperately trying to act "normal". That was a truly irie stoned.'

Ali loves that wibbly-wobbly feeling. 'I even used to enjoy that thing that most people hate about dope-smoking and drinking, when you lay your head back and the room spins,' he says. 'I actually got off on that!'

From that time we knew weed was for us. Some of us tried other types of drugs, black bombers, Mandrax, all that stuff, but only once or twice. 'One of the reasons none of us were ever tempted by heroin was because a bunch of kids who were part of our circle got heavily into it,' says Ali. 'We watched people jack up into abscesses in their groins, so saw first-hand how vile it was. All those people are dead now.'

In between heroic bouts of dope-smoking, Ali, Jimmy and Earl also played along to their favourite reggae records. At first rudimentary, the three of them eventually found their rhythmic grasp improving and after a few more months, just before Christmas 1978, they again invited Robin along to hear them play.

Robin had been supplementing his income playing snooker for money, since he had completely lost faith in his and Duncan's second-hand car business. On his way to the rehearsal he decided to go for broke, and bought a left-handed Fender Stratocaster for £210 from Musicland in Birmingham. 'This was when everyone was talking about taking up an instrument,' he recalls. 'This guitar had a horrible sunburst finish and a Union Jack scratchplate. I removed the neck and the scratchplate and applied this stuff which takes off the paint job.

'Using a scraper I started to strip it down and, at the point where the neck goes into the body, I found written into the wood the surname of the person who made the guitar: Campbell.

'I scraped a bit more and there was the initial: R.

'As more and more paint came off, I saw the year the guitar was made: 1954. The year I was born and also — I later found out — the year Fender first started making Strats.

'The hairs stood up on the back of my neck. I was stunned.

It felt as though I was meant to play the guitar. That was the message: maybe I should be doing this.

'I repainted the guitar and at UB40's second gig this geezer in the audience offered me £500 for it, but I turned him down. I've still got it.

'That guitar will never leave me.'

When Robin got to the rehearsal it was evident that Ali, Jimmy and Earl were deadly serious. 'I was amazed. Now they were making music, whereas before it wasn't even close,' says Robin. 'I could actually hear tunes being played, with all the instruments in time with each other! We stood in the garden afterwards chatting about it, and I asked my mate Mel and my brother Duncan what they thought. They snorted. "Naaah. It ain't gonna happen, is it?"

'I said to Duncan, "What else are we going to do? We can't sell cars and keep on scratching around snooker halls for money." I tried to persuade Duncan to join as well, but he wasn't up for it, even though he loves his reggae and grew up with it, just like us two.

'So I decided I was in, even if Dunc wasn't. I knew I had found the answer. This was why I couldn't hold jobs down or take the blue coat, because music was what I really wanted to do.'

This decision dealt the final hammer blow to Robin's marriage. 'I took my guitar and stereo and said to Sally, "I'm off with Ali and the rest of his mates in the band." She was brilliant about it. There were a couple of times when she tried to persuade me back, but Sally also knew it was the right thing for both of us. She was doing her thing, and enjoying it, and I was going off to go around England in the back of a van.'

The band was dedicated to practising five days a week so Robin promptly joined the rest of us on the dole. We'd decided to treat the band like a full-time job. Signing-on meant that we had to turn up for every rehearsal at nine in the morning.

From the off, Ali had been insistent that the band should have no lead vocalist, instead concentrating on performing purely instrumental dub music. He was definite that under no circumstances would he be the singer.

'I started listening to reggae as it went through the changes in the 60s, through ska and bluebeat,' explains Robin. 'But Ali's formative years were in the 70s when dub came to the fore, so he was into all those records, Lee Perry's *Black Ark in Dub* and Sly & Robbie's *Dutchman Dub*. We quickly told him the idea of a strictly dub band was stupid. It was ridiculous not to have a singer – especially since his voice was so strong – and in the end he gave in.'

Ali's unique vocal style was already fully developed. 'I'd been singing since I was a little kid,' he says. 'I loved Michael Jackson, Stevie Wonder and Bob Marley and sang along to their records constantly. By the time I was twelve, before me balls had dropped, I could sing them perfectly. I think we must get it from our old man; Rob and I have never found it difficult to sing in tune, and harmonies come very easily to us.'

The others quickly came on board: our friend Jimmy Lynn was our first keyboard player, if you can call him that: he played a Stylophone stuck through a fifteen-watt amp.

Once we had some equipment, we went through that winter building up a set of our own reggae songs at Trafalgar Road.

Then Duncan decided to try his hand as a croupier in Bournemouth. He had been living in a flat in Showell Green Lane in Moseley, so Ali and Jimmy moved in and promptly robbed the meters. Soon they were joined by Earl's brother, Ray 'Pablo' Falconer, who went on to become our first soundman. With Robin living around the corner in College Road, the only people who had to travel to rehearsals were Norman, who lived a few miles away in Northfield, while Mickey – when he came to replace Jimmy Lynn – was a similar distance away in Edgbaston.

There's a photograph somewhere of all of us huddled in the garden at Trafalgar Road, covered in snow, taken in that bitter winter of 1978/9. Brian has a big ginger Afro and Robin's got long hair and a flat tweed cap. Jimmy's wearing the grey Tonik jacket which was part of the suit bought for Ali when he worked at Butlin's. We cut the collar down because it sported those embarrassingly huge 70s lapels.

For a while the band's joke name was Jeff Cancer and the Nicoteenies. This was the punk era remember! And then our friend Andy Nash mentioned all the dole forms we were constantly signing. The official name for them was Unemployment Benefit Form Number 40, so Andy said, 'You're all on the dole, why don't you call yourselves UB40?'

We thought that was brilliant and started to bombard Birmingham with the name, writing it on walls and putting up stencils and fly posters at night. Soon, everywhere you looked in the inner city, you'd see our name. One time, before we had even played our first gig, we were in the Fighting Cocks, the happening pub in Moseley, and heard these kids at the bar. One said to the other, 'Have you heard UB40?'

The reply? 'Yeah – they're a great band.'

7

First Steps

Billed as 'jazz-dub-reggae', our first gig was on the back of a lorry at the Moseley Festival in early 1979, where we played the five compositions we had been working on.

'It was brilliant and ridiculous at the same time!' says Ali. 'We were on the back of this moving vehicle falling all over the place as we went round and round the streets playing the same set over and over again. There were loads of friends and family there supporting us, so it was quite an experience. Our parents were proud though Dad wasn't impressed at our levels of musicianship initially.'

Around that time we were particularly spurred on by a visit to a gig at Birmingham College of Food and Domestic Arts by the Coventry Automatics, soon to spearhead the 2-Tone movement as the Specials. For us lovers of reggae, they were the worst band we had ever seen. It was infuriating that these punks were ruining ska, and we marched straight back to rehearsals and drilled the songs time and time again to ensure that, when it came to it, we would be able to do justice to our beloved music. Although we all loved the rocksteady and ska which inspired the 2-Tone set, we felt it was natural to move on and perform reggae in a contemporary way.

'I remember telling Dad that we had some gigs lined up; Jimmy Lynn had organised a support tour with local punk band the Prefects,' says Ali. 'Dad said, "But you can't play your instruments!" I told him "We'll learn." and his response was: "Fuck off and don't be ridiculous."'

For the first three months or so our 'manager' was this bloke Peg Leg Steve, so named because he did actually have a wooden leg. He might have had something to do with Jimmy Lynn, but exactly how he came to manage us is lost in the mists of time. Then out of the blue arrived our first proper manager, Simon Woods, introduced to us by a mutual friend Lindy (Belinda Short). Simon was a cockney bloke who hung out on the Moseley scene and had been an encyclopaedia salesman.

One day he came to see us rehearse in the Trafalgar Road cellar and – romantically enough – introduced himself by saying, 'Hi guys, I'm an ex-junkie and I'm twenty-four.' That meant he was the same age as Rob, but to the rest of us he seemed incredibly worldly-wise.

Simon had been among the crowd at our first proper gig, which took place on 9 February 1979 at the Hare and Hounds in King's Heath at what has become known in UB40's history as the Varty Party, because it was for the birthday of this girl who was part of the Moseley crowd, Sue Varty. Also on the bill were a bunch of punk and new-wave bands we knew from the Moseley scene, including the Au Pairs, the Denizens and Pretty Faces.

Anybody who was anybody in the music scene in our part of the Midlands was there, even a pre-Culture Club Boy George, who had moved up to live in Walsall with his friend Martin Degville, later the frontman of 80s shockers Sigue Sigue Sputnik. 'I clearly remember George and Martin walking around the Bull Ring and the roughest punk clubs in all sorts of weird regalia,' says Robin. 'You had to admire their gall, done up in dresses, make-up and mad hair like geisha girls. Once Martin strolled past a bunch of really heavy skinheads with a full birdcage surrounding his head. He didn't blink once. George stood out in any crowd, a tall geezer in a big fluffy coat and a giant hat with feathers stuck into it.'

There were also people from the Brum fashion trade like Jane Kalm and Patti Bell, who ran a stall in the Oasis market with Martin Degville and was married to Birmingham rocker Steve Gibbons. And there were also loads and loads of our friends, who were so excited to see us play at last after all the rehearsing and all the self-hyping.

The crowd at the Varty Party went mental at our performance but, looking back, we were probably pretty pathetic, mainly because we'd never played through a PA before, and took it far too seriously. All of us were shaking with nerves.

However, the day after the Varty Party we knew that we had something. We were the talk of the town, or rather Moseley village, and then things started to gather pace when Simon Woods moved into the Showell Green Lane squat where Ali, Jimmy and Earl lived.

After just one more gig – supporting a band called Iganda at Birmingham University – Yomi left. Or rather, was removed. The immigration authorities sent him back to Nigeria. He would never have lasted in the band; he and Jimmy Lynn had already fallen out in a big way, resulting in Jimmy leaving the band as well. To be honest, we all gave a big sigh of relief when that happened. Jimmy was a good guy, really enthusiastic, but he was always a bit too much for some of us.

Jimmy's replacement was this guy Mickey Virtue, who we also knew from the Moseley crowd. Mickey wasn't only crucial to the future of UB40, he reintroduced Ali to his sister, Bernie. They had gone out with each other for a year and a half when Ali was still at Moseley School of Art.

'We started seeing each other again and soon enough she

moved into my room at the Showell Green Lane squat,' says Ali. 'Not long after she became pregnant with our eldest, Ali Jr, and we moved to a nearby block of flats. We lived together for twelve years in all before we married.'

By this time Robin was in a relationship with Nicky one of the gaggle of very early fans who used to watch us rehearse. 'Nicky was around a lot,' says Robin. 'We'd have a drink in the Fighting Cocks or wherever, and soon we started seeing each other.'

The upstairs front room at Showell Green Lane became our new rehearsal studio and Simon worked on getting us live work. Our third proper gig was to be our worst ever: Mount Pleasant Community Centre. We did it to raise money for our branch of the Claimants' Union, though there wasn't much of an audience at Mount Pleasant that night.

Those that were there were mainly from other bands like Fashion, the Wide Boys and the Au Pairs, so were hypercritical. There were also some pretty hardcore black kids who expressed their disapproval at our performance by playing the piano at the other end of the hall. While we were on stage. That's how bad we were.

Mount Pleasant was one of the only two times in our entire career that we fell apart on stage and gave up the gig as a dead loss. The other was when we played the Little Hall at Digbeth and smoked a bong before we went on. We were useless that night, and vowed never again to smoke one of those before a performance.

But it was good to get those experiences under our belt right at the start of our career. We made damn sure we were never as sloppy again.

Another night, at Digbeth Civic Hall – which years before had been where Grandad took the tickets for the wrestling and had been the site of the old man's club, the Jug – we played along-side the Au Pairs and some other new-wave bands. The Angelic Upstarts had been on the bill but didn't show up, so there were some pretty angry skinheads in the crowd.

'That was the first time I'd ever witnessed a crowd rush the stage,' says Robin. 'There were kids flying through the air, grabbing mike stands and anything else they could lay their hands on.'

After this, as 1979 turned to spring, the gigs kept coming and the crowds outside the venues grew and grew, though we continued to be stony-broke because there was not a lot of money coming in to share between the nine of us, including Simon Woods.

We played a few Rock Against Racism benefits, the Saltley Festival and pubs such as the Fighting Cocks. Then we had a residency for a few weeks at the New Inns on Moseley Road, Balsall Heath, which is where the final piece of the UB40 jigsaw – Astro – first witnessed us live.

Astro had been working with Duke Alloy's sound system around the Birmingham reggae dances, and knew a lot of the same kids we had grown up with. Duke Alloy had even played the Jug when we ran the Friday night reggae club. When Astro came back to Showell Green Lane after one of the New Inns shows we all got along so well it was decided there and then he should join as our MC, encouraging the audiences to dance. Soon he was toasting over the instrumental sections of our songs, in his inimitable British style. The fly-posting and wall-spraying campaign had such an effect that by the time of the New Inns residency, there were huge crowds of people outside every time we played. Ranking Roger, who was just about to join the Beat and had bright orange hair at the time, even jumped up on stage and joined us for a gig there. There is a brilliant piece of film of us performing with him. It looks straight out of the Cavern.

'It was around then I was finally thrown off the dole,' says Ali. 'They told me that if I didn't get a job I would be sent to a rehabilitation centre in Henley-in-Arden, weaving baskets. Rather than do that me and Mickey Virtue started working nights at the Cadbury's chocolate factory in Bournville. We lasted all of seven weeks. It was a totally frightening experience. Most of our fellow workers were Polish, and had been working nights at the factory ever since the end of the war. They were like something out of *Metropolis* or an Orwellian nightmare. A lot of them were doing amyl nitrate to keep them going through the night. Unreal.'

By the time Mickey and Ali gave up their jobs at Cadbury's the whole 2Tone business was kicking off, particularly in the Midlands. In the wake of punk a lot of people had gone back to the 60s music from which reggae developed: ska and bluebeat. They also picked up on the style of the original rude boys: pork-pie hats, skinny ties, loafers and tight three-button suits, and the Specials' 2Tone label became a focal point for a whole movement. As reggae fanatics we were genuinely annoyed by the whole ska thing because it seemed so backward-looking, though we personally liked the guys in other bands such as the Specials and Madness. However, we also recognised that 2Tone would help open doors for us, so we played a few more gigs in other parts of the country, including a support slot at the Electric Ballroom in Camden Town for Madness and the Beat. The Beat were from Brum as well and had recently scored a Top Ten hit with their cover of 'Tears of a Clown'. 'The Beat used to support *us*, they'd started as fans of ours,' says Robin. 'I remember congratulating their singer, Dave Wakeling, and he said to me, "Don't worry, it'll happen for you."'

It was really exciting to be playing in London but the show turned into a fairly typical event for those times, with skinheads rushing the stage. The venue held about two thousand kids, and at one point they all went to the back of the hall and then just stormed ahead, surging onto the stage. There were kids being crushed to fuck and us kicking wave upon wave of them back onto the floor. We didn't have any security with us but with our crew we made up a posse of about twenty who weren't going to take any shit. It was all fairly harmless. At the Electric Ballroom they even made the audience members take their boots off before they entered the hall.

The scene in the Midlands was moving very fast at that point, spurred on by the fuss about 2Tone and the Specials, Selecter, the

Beat and Dexy's Midnight Runners. 'I think everybody expected us to make at least one single for 2Tone, because everything released on the label at the time became a hit,' says Robin. 'Jerry Dammers of 2Tone had offered us the opportunity, but we didn't want to be part of that movement. We considered ourselves to be a reggae band, not revivalists concentrating on music which, by that stage, was a decade old. Even though we would have been ensured a hit on 2Tone, we knew it would be a backward move musically so we said no. We were also arrogant enough to assume we would have a Top Ten hit soon anyway.'

In the histories of the Midlands music scene there's a story about a massive punch-up between us and Dexy's at a house party given by one of the girls from the Au Pairs. It sounds really good, with all eight of us lined up against the nine of them, but the fact is only Mickey represented UB40 when it all kicked off.

We had all been there but left Mickey to it, sitting on the couch rolling joints. Some time after we'd left a brick was lobbed through the window and Mickey became embroiled, grabbing Dexy's singer Kevin Rowland by the hair and booting him in the nose. Somebody – possibly a Dexy – cut Mickey's hand to make him let go, and that was that.

A year later we made our first appearance on *Top of the Pops* alongside Dexy's. Kevin Rowland was blowing kisses at us from the audience while we were lip-synching, and the drummer, Stoker, who fancied himself and was pretty wide at the top, was coming on quite strong.

'In the corridor at the *Top of the Pops* studios Stoker and I were walking towards each other,' says Robin. 'Every time he went one way, I moved to block him. Eventually he slunk past and I went, "Wanker!"

'I met a grown up Stoker years later and he was very pleasant and altogether apologetic, as Kevin Rowland has been. All we can say is: apologies accepted.'

Although it was brilliant to be out on the road, some of the venues were pretty crappy. The Factory in Manchester – run by Tony Wilson, who also had Factory Records and became famous through the film based on his life, *24 Hour Party People* – was not only a right shithole but also a very depressing place to play. On the drive up, there we were, stuck in a Luton van with slush pouring in through the leaky floor. Then we were sweating like bastards on stage. And several hours later we'd be dropped off back in Brum, walking home in the freezing cold morning, all for next to no money, wondering why the hell we had bothered.

Around that time we received some much-needed support from the very nice – though slightly eccentric – Dave Cox, who was a butcher by trade and a philanthropist in the true sense of the word. He was later a Liberal MP and is now a poultry farmer, but at the time he struck a deal with Simon Woods and lent us a lot of money which sustained us through the early years, funding our tours and keeping many wolves from the door.

'Dave Cox is a lovely guy,' says Ali. 'We could never quite understand why he put so much faith in us, but he let us rehearse in the back of his shop and would come along to see us play and film our shows. He was also a great friend of Brian's, who had worked for him as a Saturday boy at his butcher's shop, and Simon Woods knew of his generosity.'

Dave was famous locally for looking after his staff. There were about eight guys working for him and he would let them use his flat, lend them money, just see they were alright. He lent us cash without condition, saying, 'Don't worry about it. Give it back to me when you've got it.' When we received our first cheque from the record company a year or so later it amounted to £70,000. We paid all of that money to our debtors, the principal one being Cllr Cox.

God bless you, Alderman.

In our early days there were several acts of generosity which were key not only to our survival but also to our eventual success. Once we opened for Nick Lowe and Dave Edmunds and their band Rockpile at a college gig. Rockpile's manager, Jake Riviera, who had run Stiff Records and also managed Elvis Costello, told Brian after the show that he thought we were great. He asked Brian if there was anything we needed in particular, and Brian told him about the rubbish sax he had to play. Jake asked Brian how much a new Selmer Mk II would cost. When Brian told him it would be around £700, he handed over the cash, there and then, saying, 'Give it to me when you've got it.' A couple of years later we played Elvis Costello's Christmas Party at Birmingham NEC. Elvis thought he had made the smart move by putting us last on the bill after he had performed, since the transport would be finished by that time. But what happened? Because we were local heroes by that time, the Brummie authorities decided to hold the buses and trains for our audience and everybody stayed. The place was rammed and we stole the show. That was a mega-gig in UB40's history since it was also the first time we played the NEC.

Anyway, back in the early days – amid the most welcome acts of generosity – we also knocked on a lot of doors touting demo tapes we had recorded at the studios in Brum owned by reggae band Steel Pulse. They had released the *Handsworth Revolution* album, and were big-time as far as we were concerned, so recording there was a bit intimidating.

Some of the tracks recorded in Handsworth were sent to the late, lamented John Peel, who played them and gave us our first national radio exposure.

'Me and Rob hitchhiked to Banbury in Oxfordshire to see Dave Swarbrick of Fairport Convention, who had been in Dad's band,' Ali recalls. 'His missus had worked for Island Records and knew the owner Chris Blackwell very well. Apparently Blackwell listened to the tape and then pronounced that we had "no commercial viability whatsoever".'

We also went along to see Erskine Thompson, he of the Diskery where our brother Dave had worked years before. 'He told us to meet him in the changing rooms of his squash club,' remembers Ali. 'He came out with a towel round his neck, wearing nothing else, absolutely stark bollock naked. Any discussion about our music seemed pointless under the circumstances, so we left.'

By this time we were desperate to get a record out, and had received some interest from the majors. They made pretty standard offers, based on advances and royalty rates of between 8 and 12 per cent. Chrysalis Records had even promised us £150,000 up front, but the royalty rate was peanuts and we knew that the figures wouldn't sustain a band with eight members. 'Because of Dad's experience of the music industry, and because of the general mindset of the band, we knew that the better the deal to start with, the more money we would earn in the future,' says Robin. 'The majors will always give you money up front, that big carrot, but you never get a slice of the cake in the end. That was what we were after, total artistic control and a big slice of the cake, the kind of slice every band should be getting.'

Then Simon Woods struck a deal with Dave Virr, who ran a minuscule indie record label called Graduate with his wife Sue from their record shop above Theedham's hardware store in Dudley High Street.

The Graduate shop had been around for a while, specialising in rare imported vinyl, especially Northern Soul, and Dave had put some stuff out on the label, scoring a minor indie hit with a version of Chris Spedding's 'Motor Bikin'' by a bunch of Brummie heavy metallers called Eazie Ryder.

It didn't seem the most likely home for UB40, but the deal was dead right for us. Although there was no cash advance it gave us total control over what songs we recorded and released. Under the terms of the contract Graduate would pay for the cost of recording and manufacturing our first album, in return for which we got 50 per cent of all revenues.

That is now the standard independent recording deal, but at the time there was barely an indie label scene, and certainly no other band had that kind of arrangement. It was also crucial for us to have complete artistic control. 'Our line was: you, the label, make and distribute our records but we don't want anybody telling us what kind of music to make or dictating to us in any way,' says Robin. 'When Dave met our demands we got him to draw up a two-page contract – these days they can run to a hundred or so pages – and we promptly signed it.'

The contract also stipulated that the album would be produced by a character called Bob Lamb, one of the Moseley crowd who had been the drummer in local Birmingham rockers the Steve Gibbons Band, who'd scored a hit with 'Tulane' in 1977.

'We saw Bob as a wise person who had been there and done it,' says Ali. 'He looked like a typical 70s rocker with longish hair, check shirt, belt with a big buckle, lots of denim and cowboy boots. He'd even toured with the Who.' Bob was a nice, laid-back guy who was very popular and threw great parties. He had also ploughed his money into a little demo studio which was used by a lot of the Moseley bands. As part of the deal Bob was to receive a 25 per cent share of royalties accrued from the album. That's how the track '25%' came about. We were so incensed that the producer would receive that much in comparison with our 6.25 per cent each that we wrote an instrumental about it!

Although we adopted our usual arrogant attitude, we were actually dead excited with the idea of finally committing our own songs to tape, because we believed that once the wider world heard them we would be on our way. We were always confident about this, but even we understimated how big it would become.

8

Signing Off

So, in the late summer of 1979, we all crammed into the tiny eight-track studio in Bob Lamb's converted flat. In reality it was no more than a bedsit with a makeshift recording room attached.

Robin and his girlfriend Nicky even moved into a little flat above Bob's. 'Bob was very good at his job because he was so laid-back,' says Robin. 'There were very few people who could handle us at the time because there were eight of us firing on all cylinders and desperate to start recording properly. There would be eight pairs of hands all over his little mixing desk. We were a right handful, pretty cocky and not that impressed because it wasn't really a proper studio. If they had stuck us in one of the major studios maybe we would have been overawed. Still, Bob was great; we couldn't panic him.' It soon became clear that what we were putting down was of better quality than standard demo material. Bob told Graduate's Dave Virr he could produce a full-on proper album if another eight-track was made available. Dave supplied that and we were off and running.

We had a complete set by this point, mainly our own songs

and covers such as Randy Newman's 'I Think It's Gonna Rain Today' and Billie Holiday's 'Strange Fruit', which eventually appeared on the 12" EP included with the album. We decided to call the record *Signing Off*, since that is exactly what we had done.

'I've always started writing lyrics, but still find it difficult to complete a song on my own,' says Ali, who contributed to many of the tracks on the first album. 'I come up with all of the melodies, and add lyrical ideas, lines, couplets, choruses, that sort of thing. Usually either Robin, Jimmy or Brian will take those and create a complete song. Even so, Astro, Earl and Norman have all contributed to songs, and written their own over the years.' Among our first songs was 'Burden of Shame'. In this case, the melody was written by Ali to a bassline of Earl's, but it turned out later that it was exactly the same as four bars of the Van Morrison song 'Moondance', which Ali had never even heard at that point. We just didn't listen to music like that. After 'Burden of Shame' appeared on the album later that year, Van successfully sued us for £7,000. It was one of those things which we didn't even bother disputing, because, although we hadn't appropriated it from Van The Man, it was recognisably the same four bars and so it was his copyright by law.

'A couple of years later I bumped into him backstage at a gig in Ireland,' says Ali. 'I'd had a few and went over and remonstrated with him. "What's the matter with you? Why did you sue us?!" He muttered, "It does sound like it, though, doesn't it?" That took the wind out of my sails. I ended up going, "Well yeah, you're right I suppose. . ."'

The sessions for what became *Signing Off* were a joy; the sun was shining and, although it was just a flat crudely sectioned off into a control room and recording space, to us it felt like a real studio. We put Norman out in the garden because the room was so small he couldn't fit into it with the rest of us. Also he played his percussion instruments so loudly that we couldn't hear ourselves if he was inside!

The truth is we didn't really know how to play along with each other at the time. Brian's sax was in a different key and we didn't understand how to tune Earl's bass. But Bob Lamb did a great job with what he had, and it stands up today, twenty-five years later, in which time it has sold ten million-plus copies. If you listen carefully you can hear traffic and birds cheeping in the background, stuff which would never make it in the sterile confines of a proper studio, and that all adds to the vibe.

Even then, during those first sessions, everybody in the band expressed their own strongly held opinions, just as they do to this day. That must be horrible for the people working with us. A sound engineer will be told to do something by one of us, and then another UB will come into the studio and tell him to do something totally different.

That's one of the reasons why we don't work with producers. There have been rare occasions when some band members – namely Brian and Jimmy – have come near to being convinced that we should, but nobody can handle our music better than ourselves. We know what we're trying to achieve and a producer would take us in the wrong direction.

We've had wicked Jamaican stars mix us – Sly and Robbie, all the dons worked on 2002's *Fathers of Reggae* album – and although we were very pleased with the results there wasn't one track we couldn't have mixed better ourselves.

For a long time, beginning with *Signing Off*, we started by first laying down the drums and bass. Later those instruments were computer-generated. That meant we had a great bass player and a great drummer, neither of whom wanted to play their instruments! This dictated how albums were made and created a lot of bloody hard work in terms of coming up with melodies to suit the arrangements.

Ever since *Signing Off*, the final call on UB40 is made by the people who make it through to the end of writing, demo-ing, recording, producing, mixing and mastering. It's usually the same two or three people who have the patience to see through what can be a really tortuous process. 'I actually love sitting at the desk, day in and day out, while things are coming together,' says Robin.

There are several nervous breakdowns littering the history of UB40, mainly among those people in studios who ended up stressed beyond belief by having to work with eight very different individuals who all have the capacity to behave like lunatics. One engineer made himself very unpopular with his habit of picking flakes of coke out of his nose and eating them. He went potty when he found that one of us had reduced the back of his expensive leather jacket to ribbons with a sharp scalpel. Some of the band members thought that was hilarious but he failed to see the funny side. Another time, during a session at the BBC Studios in Maida Vale, the producer we were working with dropped off to sleep with his mouth open (the cheeky bastard) and minutes later some of the band were competing to flick cigarette ends into his mouth.

And this mad behaviour started right from the off. In the early days at least two engineers deserted their posts and refused to finish the mixes of the records they were working on. One of them was found in a state of near-catatonia in his flat saying over and over again that he couldn't handle the demands of all eight of us and do his job any more. Apparently he hadn't bathed for several days.

The early gigs in London in the late autumn of 1979 represented a really wild time. Believe it or not, a lot of people from Birmingham don't travel down there even though it's only an hour or so on the train. We'd been down on school trips to the Imperial War Museum or wherever, but decided to launch an assault on the capital by playing a tour of London venues only. We slept on various floors and stayed in squats with punk rockers, because Jimmy Lynn had moved down and had a lot of connections.

One night Jimmy got involved in a scrap with Steve Strange during a gig at the 101 Club in Clapham. We stole a couple of barrels of beer and some stage lights from the venue but received a message that if they weren't returned there'd be some real trouble. A couple of days later our roadies took them back.

The evening after the 101 Club kerfuffle we piled down the stairs of the tiny Rock Garden in Covent Garden. After the show, among the visitors into the horrible little toilet at the back they called the dressing room was none other than Chrissie Hynde, who was number one at the time with the Pretenders' hit 'Brass in Pocket'. She had come along with her bass player, Peter Farndon.

We were all very embarrassed about the surroundings and the fact that we were so sweaty and grimy after the gig, and apparently she felt pretty intimidated and at first spoke only to Brian because he seemed the most congenial. She later said that she couldn't understand a word we were saying because of our accents. Maybe that's why we get along so well! Chrissie announced that she loved our music and, right there and then, invited us to become the support on the Pretenders' UK tour, starting in just a few days.

It seemed unbelievable to us, but we immediately said, 'Of course Ms Hynde. Nothing would give us greater pleasure!'

We knew that this was our time, so we just got up there and delivered night after night and had a great tour. We'd only done about thirty gigs by that point and this was a 25-date tour of pretty reasonably sized venues: Brighton Top Rank Suite, Keele University, audiences of about two or three thousand people. And we went down really well, even to the leather-jacketed crowd. There were even occasions when we blew the Pretenders offstage.

They were a great bunch of people, three rockers from Hereford and Chrissie, who is lovely, a woman of strong convictions who we've always found to be a complete pussycat. To us the Pretenders seemed like real pop stars, but they were always funny and friendly. Within a couple of years the other two original members, Pete Farndon and James Honeyman-Scott, were to die within nine months of each other just when the band was hitting its stride. But it really came as no surprise to us since they were bang into speedballs – heroin and coke together. James was killed by a cocaine-induced heart attack in the summer of 1982 and by the following April Pete was dead from a heroin overdose.

After each show Chrissie would hang with us, so we partied – drinking and smoking together. She had experienced this really quick rush of success, with her second single going straight to number one, and liked us because we were relatively normal.

We still see drummer Martin Chambers occasionally, and even though we're over the period when we just get drunk and cry about those two being dead, it's still a terrible shame. Jimmy was only twenty-four when he went and Pete was just twenty-six. We used to think they were so much older than us but they were just babies really.

'They were roughly the same age as me,' says Robin. 'But they seemed like grown-ups. I'd retarded myself by hanging out with a bunch of twenty-year-olds and here was James in his red rockabilly suit with a big stetson and Pete in his leathers. They looked like the real thing.'

All of the band were incredibly friendly, but we didn't think much of their tour manager. Support bands often receive the shitty end of the stick from tour managers, being rushed through soundchecks to ensure that you don't come across as well as the main act, that sort of thing. Our rider – the food, drink, towels and other stuff you request for your dressing room – wouldn't turn up, but rather than let it lie, we'd report it to Chrissie and the boys, who would sort it out immediately.

But as the tour dates flew by, the veneer came off. One night in Glasgow Pete was nearly beaten to a pulp by the bouncers because he had kicked one of them while on stage, pretending to be a tough guy. The bouncers came after him once the show was over, so all of us lined up in front of Pete and told them, 'If you want him, you'll have to go through us.'

These geezers were absolutely huge, and, although we were a young gang who had been in plenty of scrapes, they could have easily walked through us. We felt honour bound to defend Pete, even though he had behaved like a prat and nearly shat his pants when it looked like the bouncers were going to have him.

We filled the corridor and told the bouncers, 'We know he's out of order, but he's really sorry and we can't let this happen. If you're going to have a go then you'll have to take us on as well.' They went, 'You lot are alright,' and let it drop. Ever since then we have always had a great welcome from security staff when we play Glasgow.

Even when we were touring with the Pretenders we didn't indulge in the rock 'n' roll lifestyle, but were strictly ganja. We had a rule that if any of our crew were found with anything but weed, we would fuck them off. One night, at the Cardiff Top Rank, Jimmy Honeyman-Scott and his pal, another famous guitarist, burst into our dressing room asking for coke. We offered them some draw but they weren't interested. Then Jimmy's mate spotted a can of Sure anti-perspirant spray on the dressing-room table and they took turns sticking the nozzle up their hooters and inhaling deeply as the spray was released! We sat back absolutely flabbergasted, but – all purple-eyed – they seemed content with that, sighed loudly and went on their way.

While we'd been on the road the sessions we'd recorded with Bob Lamb started to bear fruit. Local Brum DJ Robin Valk broadcast some of the tracks on his BRMB show, which led to a session with John Peel just before Christmas 1979. That went out in the New Year, when we also made our television debut on a local – and now long-forgotten – arts magazine show called *Mainstream*.

The Graduate label didn't know what had hit them. Within a

matter of weeks we'd toured large venues with one of the biggest bands in the UK, recorded for John Peel and started to receive attention not only from radio and TV but also the music press.

In March 1980 our debut single, 'King/Food for Thought', was released and stayed in the charts for thirteen weeks, reaching the number four spot. We shot the video in a theatre in London, dressed in the Fred Perrys and other clothes popular among the 2Tone set. We weren't chasing that scene; those were just the clothes which were fashionable among working-class people.

Whatever the attention we were getting and the chart placing of that debut single, there were already cracks beginning to appear in our relationship with Graduate. Although we were very proud of being 'truly independent' by signing with them, in hindsight it was a foolish move. We were selling loads more copies of our records than other bands, but because most of them were with major record labels whose releases went through chart shops, our success wasn't truly reflected by our chart positions.

Most bands would have been happy with their debut single reaching number four – especially in those days when you really had to shift thousands upon thousands of records to even make the Top Ten – but we knew 'King/Food for Thought' should have earned the number one spot.

Despite this, life was fantastic. We were all in our early twenties and, after just a year of putting in our dues on the road, we were on *Top of the Pops* on the night Dexy's Midnight Runners did 'Geno', while others like the Lambrettas were doing their version of 'Poison Ivy'. That was the scene then: crap mod!

'It was a lovely time in our lives; there were girls everywhere, hanging around outside our houses and trying to smash the doors down to get at us,' says Ali, who was voted Most Fancied Male in *Smash Hits* magazine, where he confessed to owning a Toyota Starlet and having had a childhood crush not only on Olivia Newton-John, but also on George Best.

We also started to headline our own tours, and quickly gained a reputation for trouble. If the tour manager was given the usual runaround by the promoter or venue operator over money – the excuse usually centred on having lost money on the tickets so that we couldn't be paid – all eight of the band and our crew would march into the back room and demand, 'Give us our fucking money.'

And you know what? Suddenly the money that hadn't been there would be found. That attitude earned us a reputation for troublemaking while all we were doing was standing up for ourselves, and we still do. Not that long ago, in the early 90s, we played a pop festival in Switzerland where the security beat up our merchandiser and took all the cash and our stock.

We tooled up with scaffolding poles and the like from the stage and paid them a visit. They had Dobermanns snarling at us on leashes. We told them, 'If you let any of them go they're dead.' They soon backed off and returned what was ours.

In 1980, our first European date was as support to Eddie Grant for a show in the main bullring in Ibiza. Thirty of us – including partners and kids – were flown over and promised a no-expenses-spared holiday with accommodation in 'beautiful new apartments' for a few days. That would set us up nicely for the gig, we thought.

Not long after we arrived we realised something was up. The bus ferrying us to those apartments took for ever. It was only when we got out that we realised that the promoter had plastered the bus with posters advertising the gig and driven round and round the island with us on board in a cheapskate attempt to rustle up some interest.

The 'beautiful new apartments' turned out to be unfinished; they were even installing window frames when we arrived and most rooms had no panes of glass for the duration of our stay. Food was also scarce. 'We were there for five nights with nothing to eat and no money,' says Robin. 'I was the only one with a credit card, which I hadn't actually used for eighteen months, so that paid for some meals, but by the time of the gig we were starving and very unhappy.'

When he demanded money upfront, our manager Simon was stonewalled; it looked to us like the promoter, an Italian, was a mobster with no intention of paying up. On the night of the show Simon told us, 'I'm going up to get the cash. Don't go on stage until you see me with the money.'

While we waited Simon had it out with the promoter, who, at one stage, pulled a gun on him. Simon told us later that he said, 'Look, if you kill me, they're definitely not going on,' and the guy relented.

The money was handed across in a brown paper bag, but the promotor called the police, because, under Spanish law he could denounce Simon and have him arrested immediately.

Simon arrived in the dressing room with the money and actually joined us on stage for the entire performance, clutching the bag while standing in between Norman and Ali.

As soon as the show was over Astro grabbed the bag and ran out of the bullring, right through the audience. We hared out of there to the airport and got the first flight, at 5a.m., to Belgium, before making our weary way home, leaving our crew and stage gear behind.

When he saw what happened, Eddie Grant refused to go on. The police were involved and he was forced to play his show the next week. As far as we know, Eddie still hasn't been paid.

When *Signing Off* came out in the autumn of 1980 it had been set up by two more Top Ten hits – 'My Way of Thinking' and 'The Earth Dies Screaming' – and was an immediate success.

One of the things which helped it along was the inclusion of the 12" EP, the recording of which we paid for out of our own pockets. The sound of the *Signing Off* sessions was too thin for us, and we noticed how the singles compared badly to, say, Bob Marley, when they were played on the radio. So we decamped to De Lane Lea Studios in London's Soho, famous for having been the venue for sessions for everybody from the Small Faces and the Stones to David Bowie and Jimi Hendrix.

It had a proper 24-track console and the improvement in the sound of songs like 'Strange Fruit' and the fittingly titled instrumental 'Reefer Madness' was huge.

The EP also featured our own song, 'Madam Medusa', which launched a vitriolic attack on Margaret Thatcher, who had been Prime Minister for a year by that point.

The lyrics were written by our dad. Originally he gave them to Robin as a present on the basis that nobody would know he was the writer. 'I told him I couldn't do that, and he said it wouldn't be a problem. When I worked them up with the band we agreed on a co-songwriting credit with him, particularly after he had already registered himself as the co-writer with the PRS, the organisation which logs songwriters!' says Robin. 'The words on that song demonstrate how wicked a songsmith our old man is.'

Signing Off went to number two and stayed in the album charts for 71 weeks. The rest of the family were really proud of our success. Dad couldn't get his hat on, he was so happy for us.

Initially the press reaction to us was friendly. Even though UB40 were supposed to be without an identifiable frontman, us brothers and Astro reluctantly became the public faces of the group. We also used to play around with the press by sending different combinations of band members from the ones they had requested, but eventually the media got wise.

'By this time I had a house back in Balsall Heath, on Brighton Road,' says Ali. 'I wanted to live where I came from, and it was literally open house. The door was always ajar and there were people around all the time, and it was the same story at Brian's, Jim's and the rest of us.

'When I look back now, I don't really know what I was playing at. It was OK while I was single and didn't have any kids, but as soon as they started to come along I wanted them to play with ferns rather than used condoms, so eventually I moved to Barnt Green, described locally as "the leafiest suburb of South Birmingham". Dad was ashamed of me. He called it "fuckin' bookie country"!'

9

Present Arms

During our time with Graduate we quickly realised that independent record companies – particularly in the early 80s – didn't have the muscle to help you get chart profile because they weren't hooked into one of the powerful majors such as EMI, CBS or WEA.

Graduate's distribution was handled by a company called Spartan, a London-based wholesaler which specialised in indie labels but didn't in fact have the clout to get us into enough of the right stores which filed their sales figures with the compilers of the record charts.

Our first British tour in our own right had been a big success with sell-out shows and great audience reaction, the only downer being when we were busted and fined in Leeds for possession. 'I was done for 5.2 grams of cannabis, which got me a £200 fine, the first of many!' grins Ali.

When *Signing Off* went gold, having sold 100,000 copies within a few weeks of release, we knew that we were onto something big. When we first struck the Graduate deal we had paid ourselves and our crew £35 a week, and after the 'King/Food for Thought' single went Top Ten we upped that to £500 a week. The fact that it had gone gold guaranteed a steady flow of income, though of course it would have to be split first with Graduate and then nine ways between ourselves and Simon Woods.

However many copies the album sold, it still didn't crack the number one spot. We were pipped first by Gary Numan and then by Kate Bush. It seemed that whatever we did, a bunch of hoolies from Brum couldn't get into pole position.

At the end of 1980 we made the decision to leave Dave and Sue's set-up at Graduate. We felt hard done by given that they were sharing fifty per cent of the income between them while the eight of us – and Simon – had to settle for the remaining fifty per cent. Added to that, 'Burden of Shame', which was about how we all share blame for the iniquity of apartheid and includes the lyric: 'And a boy in Soweto dies. . .' was deleted from the South African release of *Signing Off*. Apparently the local record company was running scared because the SA government banned the song from being sold or played on the radio.

The first we knew of 'Burden of Shame' being dropped from the South African release of *Signing Off* was during a press interview, when a journalist asked us what we thought about it.

That was the final straw. *Signing Off* had sold about a million copies by that point and, if Graduate had told us that the South Africans weren't prepared to release the album with that song on it, our response would have been: 'Fuck 'em.'

But we hadn't even been consulted. We were of the opinion that Graduate was in breach of contract, since we were supposed to have complete control over our music and which tracks appeared where. Their decision to delete 'Burden of Shame' ran counter to the agreement, and, at a meeting at Graduate, Dave and Sue Vivv broke down in tears when we told them it was over.

Around the same time we parted company with Simon Woods. We had always had a handshake agreement with him, but he proposed a new deal which would not only split our revenues fifty-fifty with him, but also earn him commission on our income as well. Putting this to us formally at a meeting, he suggested we sign there and then. Robin told him that we wanted to think about the plan overnight, and everybody agreed. His face dropped.

'That night we were all on the phone to each other,' recalls Robin. 'Ali and Norman were saying to me, "Does it read like I think it reads?" My response was, "Yeah, exactly!" I couldn't fucking believe it. Everything should have been split nine ways – i.e. equally between the members of the band and the manager. Usually a rock and roll manager receives 15 or 20 per cent but the UB40 way was, if you are a part of our posse then you receive an equal amount to us. Nothing else is acceptable. We have a gang mentality and Simon's proposed deal gave him something close to 60 per cent.'

The very next morning we told him, 'How the fuck did you think you could get that past us? Do you have such a low opinion of our intelligence? You're gone, mate. The second you bite the hand that feeds you, and demonstrate that you're not part of the posse, fuck you.' The sad thing is that – and we have witnessed this a lot over the years – it seemed to us that Simon had bought into the notion in the music business that the manager is more important than the artist.

'There had always been a bit of a gulf between us anyway,' says Ali. 'Simon and his girlfriend were part of that bohemian/arty Moseley scene, the "outerlectuals", as I called the pretentious people who weren't really our type at all.'

It was then decided that – in the short term at least – our brother David should become Simon's replacement as manager, two weeks after he came out from doing his four-and-a-half-year stretch. Dave is very eloquent and understood us. He told us, 'I'm not a careerist but I'll help you out.'

We knew we could trust Dave and he had already been involved in UB40, writing letters and press releases on our behalf. In the end he managed us for more than two years.

Around this time we joined an exclusive club: bands whose subversive activities have earned them an MI5 file. There's just us, John and Yoko, the Sex Pistols and anarcho-punks Crass who have that dubious privilege.

'It came as no surprise to me,' says Robin. 'Our old man was under surveillance in the 60s. A friend of his – a high-up engineer at the GPO – told him that that his name was on the list. Our house was bugged and phones were tapped, so we were used to it. When we became more famous than our dad, and equally as outspoken politically, it seemed reasonable to assume that we would also be targeted. And lo and behold, we were tipped off by well-wishers that we were also on the list. Playing gigs for the likes of the Autonomy anarchist group would have made them extra interested.

'It's never been out of my consciousness; I've always thought I'm being listened to on the phone, which is why I don't say very much during calls. To me a phone call isn't a private conversation. You used to be able to hear the secondary click engaging the tape machine just after you picked up the receiver.'

Since we were openly in favour of left-wing causes and the legalisation of cannabis, the situation became just like it is depicted in the movies. There'd be the usual BT vans parked outside our houses for days, and the building opposite our recording complex, was even occupied by police with cameras and notebooks for a long time.

Someone who worked in the garage underneath contacted one of our staff and said, 'You won't believe this but the whole of our top floor has been taken over by the cops. They're noting down everything, photographing every single car registration that comes in and out.'

It's difficult to know exactly what they were after. As well as the political connections, we have known a few nefarious individuals over the years. Our local pub, the Eagle & Tun – where the video for 'Red Red Wine' was shot – became a boxers' pub, the Cauliflower Ear, and we knew all the crowd from there, which may have interested the police.

But we never let the surveillance get to us. They were on a hiding to nothing and we think they dropped it a few years back, though doubtless the file is still open somewhere.

We're not sure whether Dave's 'criminal' past was a contributory factor, but anyway, after a couple of years managing us, some of the other UBs, in particular Brian, felt insecure about Dave handling the band and that was fair enough: two Campbells may be OK but three – including the manager – was probably a bit rich.

When Dave first came on board we set up our own record label, DEP International, and initially continued the distribution deal with Spartan. We knew the way forward would be to license our recordings to a major distributor with the muscle to get our music racked in record shops, which would then be properly reflected in the chart. The first of these was CBS, then flying high with everyone from the Clash to Michael Jackson on their books.

By restricting the major to a licensing deal we could maintain control, because we owned the recordings. That independence was to stand us in good stead through the good and bad times to come.

We recorded *Present Arms*, our follow-up to *Signing Off*, at Wembley Studios, not far from the football stadium. One song from those sessions proved particularly timely. 'One in Ten', our comment on the unemployment statistics, was a big hit in the riotous summer of 1981, and we became very much involved in the political situation, playing benefits for those arrested during the inner-city conflicts across the country, which in turn resulted in bans from some venues.

But even then we always tried to hold the politics at bay, because what we are, and have always been, is a band of music-makers.

Part of our mission from the earliest days was that every other album would be dub, which is exactly how our next album, *Present*

Arms in Dub, came about. We wanted to do what had been happening on the reggae scene for years: produce 'dubs' – as in alternative instrumental mixes – of the tracks on *Present Arms*.

In those days not a lot was known about dub, and of course there were complaints about the lack of vocals from the record company, but we managed to get the first dub album into the mainstream charts, so obviously it reached out to a lot of people.

We set about remixing *Present Arms* by trying to make a Jamaican dub record, but of course it didn't come out like that because we were never a Jamaican reggae act. At the same time we weren't even a proper English reggae band along the lines of Steel Pulse or Matumbi. It was really Ali's baby because he was so mad for dub in those days. We'd work hard and were uncompromising to outsiders, although, as always, we compromised between ourselves.

A lot of the fans were taken aback initially but the critical reaction was strong. And even though the sales were tiny compared to our regular albums, to this day *Present Arms in Dub* is the biggest-selling dub album ever. We're still very proud of that achievement and soon afterwards everyone, from David Bowie to Culture Club, was releasing dub mixes of their singles.

10

Cocaine in My Brain

In early 1982 we set about making the *UB44* album at Windmill Lane Studios in Dublin, the place where U2, the Stones and so many other acts have worked. Everything seemed fine. We'd had a fantastic run: *Signing Off* and *Present Arms* had spent months and months in the charts and 'One In Ten' had really established us.

It seemed nothing could go wrong. But, for the first time since we had started UB40, the personal and professional lives of the band started to take a dip and, in particular, the music began to suffer. Up to this point we had really enjoyed the process of recording, releasing, promoting and touring records, but now there was a new factor. In our early years most of the band were permanently stoned, but then cocaine kicked in, and soon enough it was party time all the time.

'*UB44* was our *Spinal Tap* moment,' says Ali. 'Check the fact that it was the first album to feature a hologram on its cover! The people who invented the process for mass-producing holographic images came to us and put themselves forward as the sleeve designers. So we commissioned them. Just like *Spinal Tap*'s Stonehenge set-up, we had large UB and 44 characters cut out of polystyrene for the album cover shoot. It costs us a fortune.'

The *UB44* sessions at Windmill Lane were pure madness. Dublin is a great city full of lovely people but the experience was depressing as the whole band – apart from Robin and Mickey – snorted vast amounts of bugle. Previously all we had cared about was draw. Only a couple of years before, we had discovered that someone in the UB40 camp had been doing coke on the sly. When we caught him snorting backstage at that gig at the Factory in Manchester there was a major confrontation, and we collectively threatened to kick him out, such was our hatred of the drug.

But then, with success, it began to appear everywhere. We hired a tour manager who was a cokehead. He'd previously worked with the Bay City Rollers, so God knows how he came to be with us, but one night on tour in Belgium he produced a quarter of a gram. We were like little boys: 'Whassat then?'

Within a matter of weeks certain members of the band and crew were snorting malaria tablets, Lemsip sachets, anything they could get their hands on. Then there was the acid, Supermans, Doves, magic mushrooms. 'We were actually into mushrooms before the band started,' says Ali. 'It was considered OK to go picking them, but when they're dry they are potent little mother-fuckers. On them I've shrunk to the size of a tiny person fearing for my life at the size of the wheels of cars, and I've also grown into a giant who can see four miles up the road.'

Soon certain members of the band was doing coke everywhere: restaurants, supermarkets, you name it. We'd always bickered, but the presence of gear made us argue all the more. In Dublin we were snorting in the studio, and that really had a bad impact. Every track we put down was too slow; it sounded like music made by people who were half-asleep. The tunes on that album are great but the execution was fucked-up. These days we can't bear to listen to tracks like 'I Won't Close My Eyes' in their original form

'It is one of our best songs, but I'm so out of tune it's unbeliev-able,' says Ali. 'Totally depressing. I loved the positive slant of

Brian's lyrics, so it's a shame we did it no justice until I remixed it a few years later.'

No surprise then that the original version broke our successful run when it was released as a single and only got to number 32. There again, everything on *UB44* was out of tune, but most of us were too out of it at the time to even notice. We'd love to have the chance to rerecord it, because there are beautiful songs buried in there somewhere.

There were tensions between us brothers, just as the tensions grew in the rest of the band. 'Robin's always been a straight geezer,' says Ali. 'He's not a big drinker and has never ever been into narcotics, but he kind of let us get on with it. After all, we were a bunch of young men doing everything you're supposed to do when you're in a successful band. It was all there on a plate and I for one definitely did everything to excess.'

For Robin, *UB44* evokes equally sad memories. 'Although I didn't say very much at the time to any of them, I was terrified of what coke was doing,' he says now. 'It felt like everybody had gone mad around me; you know what it's like when you're the only sober one at the party. You can't get on anybody else's wavelength and they can't understand you.

'What happened is that pretty soon there was a complete collapse in communication because they were so off their faces. You'd have a heated row about something and twenty minutes later that same person would be agreeing with you wholeheartedly on the very same subject. The character changes were horrible to witness, and, of course, there is nothing more boring than being the only sober person there. For someone like Ali, who was already a piss-pot by that time, coke made him drink all day and all night.'

That happened to a lot of the band. People were being dragged out of bed unconscious and literally loaded onto the bus, and the performances suffered. We once found Astro unconscious in his own puke halfway down the road from our hotel outside a little village in Italy. He'd drunk a bottle of grappa by himself in a bar for a laugh and never made it back to his room, literally passing out in a ditch on his way back.

'Cocaine enables you doesn't it?' says Ali, who quickly developed a passion for the drug which haunted him for many more years. 'It's the great consumer drug. It makes you drink and smoke four times the amount that you normally would.'

Robin admits that coke scares him. 'I've never done a line in my life,' he says. 'The only time I did it was when a band member gave me some to rub into my gums; I was in a lot of pain because I'd dislocated my jaw and couldn't get to a dentist so it eased the discomfort for a short while.'

One day Robin sat down with Earl and Jimmy and played them back a session they had recorded the day before. It was 2 p.m. and they had both just risen for the day. They couldn't tell what was wrong with the track, even though Jimmy sounded like he was pushing a drumkit down the stairs every time he did a roll and Earl was playing as though he'd just discovered the bass. But they wouldn't have any of it. They listened to the track, turned to each other and said, 'Sounds alright to me.'

Jimmy had almost turned into a member of Duran Duran by that point, putting purple streaks in his hair and hanging with all the party boys. We took the masters of *UB44* to the Townhouse Studios in London to mix the album. When our engineer, Rafe McKenna, first played the tapes he couldn't believe what he was hearing. Poor old Rafe spent a week using all his studio trickery to get it sounding halfway decent, and did a great job, but that record could never sound brilliant because it was though we recorded it with a blanket over us. Which of course we had in a way.

The worse news was that this was only the beginning. Coke would continue to ravage UB40 for at least the next decade. Added to that we were all living like pop stars by now, complete with nice houses and fast cars. Everybody moved out of the inner city.

'After my flat in Moseley I bought a house there,' says Robin. 'There was a hole in the fence through which I'd see the next-door neighbour's eye peeping when I was sitting in my front room watching the telly. That was too much for me, so eventually I moved out as well.'

There was trouble brewing for the band as a whole. CBS absolutely hated *UB44* and after an incident in France released us from our contract. One night we'd had the temerity to smoke weed during a dinner in Paris with the head of their French label. The next day we were told that our contract had been terminated because the French boss was so disgusted with our behaviour.

To be frank we couldn't blame them for cancelling the deal, though the timing could have been better; they dropped us when we were sat in the studio doing the final mixes!

Then Richard Branson came to the rescue. He expressed an interest in signing us to Virgin Records, though, we insisted that he come up to DEP on his own with no lawyers, accountants, record executives or managers present. We sat Branson in the middle of the room and quizzed him about what he could offer us. He seemed very impressive and proposed a much better deal than the one we had with CBS so we signed with Virgin, the label we were to be with for the next twenty-three years.

'As Reg Kray might have said: "I found him to be a very likeable and well-adjusted fellow",' says Ali. Branson himself has been reported as saying that he's never been so scared in a business meeting before or since.

We all knew that *UB44* wasn't the greatest of albums and it certainly wasn't a commercial success. It reached number four in the charts but didn't stay there for very long, while the singles were only Top Twenty hits at best. But out of the sense of failure surrounding the whole *UB44* experience would come the most important project of our career.

11

Crazy Limeys

Suddenly, the world opened up for us. In September 1981, after doing the usual round of gigs in Europe and Britain, we got to play a series of dates in Australia. However, those performances are still tainted with sadness for us brothers. When we played Sydney we met up again with our uncle Dave – Dad's brother who emigrated to Oz when we were in our teens. We had a party with him after one of the shows, and it turned into a fantastic family reunion over the barbie. On returning home to the UK the next day, we were greeted by UB40's business manager, Paul Davies, who told us Dave had died in a car crash while we were on the flight back.

Traversing the globe offers up a complete range of experiences, from utter boredom, tragedy, misery and sometimes fear for our lives to sheer happiness and celebration. In the summer of 1982 we were granted our first opportunity to visit Africa – an amazing experience – to help Zimbabwe celebrate the anniversary of independence from white colonial rule. That was such an honour, since Bob Marley and the Wailers had played the first Independence Day concert a couple of years earlier, so we were following in the tracks of the greatest.

Up until then we had always refused to tour for more than two weeks at a time. It was insane but we just didn't want to be away from home, so we would rush through, cramming countries into the schedule. We realised that to do Africa and everywhere else justice we would have to stretch the jaunt to six weeks, and that became the new limit for the next few years.

Arriving in Bulawayo, we went straight out to a frenzied photo shoot with the British newspapers who had followed us there. There were crowds all around us; it seemed we were already heroes there. Back in England the single 'Love Is All Is Alright' had only just squeezed into the Top Thirty but in Zimbabwe it stayed at the top of the charts for weeks and became the unofficial anthem of the celebrations.

Zimbabwe was a very different place then; we helped celebrate independence whereas the reason the England cricket team get such stick for visiting the country these days is that they are seen to be helping celebrate Mugabe's reign of terror.

'We were innocents in those days,' says Robin. 'But then again, so was everybody else. Nobody knew Mugabe was about to embark on a campaign of genocide against his own people. There was a spirit of: "We will win through". The night we played our massive outdoor gig the heavens opened. When we arrived they were experiencing a six-month drought, but once we took the stage it just poured down. And we've had that throughout our career. Anytime we play in hot countries it pisses with rain!'

The gig was very heavy. As we arrived a lot of the locals had stormed the barriers and the security guards unleashed attack dogs on them.

'There were horrendous scenes,' says Robin. 'One dog had sunk its teeth into this little guy's calf muscle; he was screaming like a child. Rather than drag the dog off, these other cops ran over and started beating the poor guy with sticks as the dog tore at him.'

We implored the guards to stop and told the officials that if they didn't, we would refuse to play. So the savagery ended, but only until the gig started and then it kicked off again.

During our few days in the country we went off on our own and explored, discovering what life was really like in Zimbabwe. The depth of poverty was incredible, and made us appreciate things we'd never given a second thought to, like new clothes, or even any clothes at all. Some of the people we met and saw seemed to own only the rags on their backs, nothing more.

We weren't guarded or escorted, and in fact we refused to attend some of the official ceremonies and workshops the government officials invited us to. We didn't want to be part of their propaganda machine.

We went on safari, where we encountered rhinos and giraffes at close quarters and also paid a visit to Matopos National Park. On top of a hill in the park is the grave of Cecil Rhodes, the founder of the brutal state of Rhodesia. There was a bunch of British press with us so naturally we took the opportunity to dance on Rhodes's grave, which felt pretty good, like the right thing to do, even though none of the papers used a single photograph of the event. We revisited Zimbabe in 1989, and it was remarkable what had been achieved in those seven years. The poverty appeared to have been addressed and at least people seemed to have clothes on their backs but already Mugabe's dictatorship was in full swing.

'When we played South Africa in 1991 apartheid was over. There was also a sense there that the people were finally in control of their lives'. says Robin. They walked with their heads held high. It was clear that the hotel we stayed in had black people among the guests, probably for the first time. There was an extraordinary atmosphere.'

It's often strange for Western musicians to visit poverty-stricken countries because it's expected that you will have a fully formed opinion about the place, having done your homework and understood all the economic and social issues. The reality is that you are just a band of travelling troubadours, there to do the gig, plain and simple. We've found that a lot of importance is attached to groups who make the effort to travel off the beaten path. Particularly if you're UB40.

Back in the summer of 1983 a revelation awaited us on our first visit to America. 'That was a real eye-opener because we smoked some Orange County buds and our lives were never the same again,' enthuses Ali. 'We had the whole deal: eyelids like earthworms and couldn't stop laughing. It was great!'

After that experience we tried to play California as often as possible because the weed wasn't as we knew it. It wasn't the commercial dirtweed we were used to here, Colombian, Thai sticks, Mexican, whatever, all full of seeds. The stuff we came across in California was buds, Sensimilla. This is before the big reggae hits such as 'Under Mi Sensi' and Black Uhuru's 'Sensimilla' but we were converted.

But we still insisted that even our American tours were restricted to six weeks, which was crazy. 'I'd be lying on the floor of the tour bus with all the air-conditioning blowers directed at me because it was so hot and I'd developed hives,' says Ali. On those stints we didn't even take overnight accommodation because it would have slowed us up. Instead we would book a single room, and jump off the bus to grab a shower before heading straight off to the gig and the next leg of the journey. Insane behaviour.

One of the reasons we were invited to play Moscow and Leningrad – as it was then – in October 1986 was because the Russians viewed us as the acceptable face of capitalism, socially aware and anti-Thatcher. In Leningrad we were booked into what was then the largest hotel in the world, a huge place with something like 3,000 rooms. There was a foul smell permeating every part of it, and we soon found out why. 'I had checked into my room and just used the toilet when there was a terrible banging at my door,' recalls Ali. 'This woman came rushing in, took one look at the bog and started berating me for having flushed toilet paper away. She gesticulated wildly that it was supposed to go in the bin!'

Before the gig the authorities asked us if we would introduce every song via a translator and explain the political significance. We turned the request down flat. We don't care where we are, UB40's job is to play music and create a show, not mount a soapbox. The organisers really couldn't understand that but the audiences knew they were there to dance and enjoy themselves.

The first rows of the stadium were made up of octogenarian members of the Politburo who would wince and put their fingers in their ears at the volume while the rest of the audience was forced to sit down. For the first few dates, anyone who stood up or danced was pushed down or received a clout. We held a meeting with the Russian tour promoter and explained that if they wouldn't let the audience dance we were going home. They came up with a bunch of excuses about fire regulations but we realised that they simply didn't understand why anybody would want to dance to a musical performance when they could sit quietly and watch.

But we got our way. After the meeting the rest of the Russian shows went off without a hitch.

After the first gig we had a major scrap with a Finnish ice-hockey team who attacked us in the hotel bar, but that was the least of it. Believe it or not, the day we arrived was the cause for much celebration: it was National Cabbage Day! The bastards were everywhere, even floating down the Volga. There were queues of people waiting to jump into the freezing waters and grab a cabbage. Unbelievable.

Arriving as we were direct from some dates in California, Russia was a shock in every way. The temperatures were subzero and we were followed everywhere by little guys pretending to read newspapers. If we spoke to anyone the authorities would consider undesirable, they'd be hustled off into a Trabant

'One night me, Brian and Pops went to a party,' says Ali. 'After taking this circuitous route to an apartment we had to give a secret knock to enter. Inside the people throwing the bash were huddled around a tiny transistor radio, reading banned books and passing around apples! It was surreal, particularly since we were suffering from a terrible come-down after California.'

An incident that occurred between us brothers during the Russian trip was to echo down the years. Already Ali's drink-fuelled behaviour was out of control, and one night in a hotel in Moscow, he became convinced that a particular woman in the band's company was out to murder him.

'He was having a paranoid attack,' sighs Robin. 'He came to tell me about it, and I tried to calm him, but the situation spun out of control. He threatened to glass me, at which point his mates dragged him up to his room. I was livid and went to talk to him, telling his pals to fuck off and leave it to us two to sort out.

'Ali was a serious mess, smashing the place up. After raging for a few minutes he broke down, apparently scared I was going to belt him for his behaviour.

'Ali sobbed, "Don't fight me, just help me." Crying his eyes out he admitted he had a problem. We agreed that the minute we got back to the UK he would go into rehab.

'At that he seemed to turn the corner, and I left him to sleep what was left of the night away. When I saw him the next morning and said that I had the number of a clinic that would take him in he asked, "What for?"

'I said, "You know. Remember what we discussed last night?"

'He said, "Fuck off! Don't be ridiculous! What do I need that for?"

'I'd been to see doctors and read books about addiction and how you help those close to you, but none of it seemed to have got through to him. After that incident in Russia I decided there was no point in talking to him about it. It was the old but true cliché: he needed to want to give up before he actually could. But it was many years before he reached that point. To this day,

Ali does not recall the incident and does not believe it took place.'

In our time we've played all around the world and back again, from the Caribbean and India to every country in South America and beyond, though borders have always been a bit of a tricky proposition for UB40. After one particular show, Ali and some of the lads crossed from Belgium into France in a flash sports car driven by his pal Jack, who kept asking them to promise they weren't holding anything which might get them all into trouble.

'We had smoked all of our shit but for some reason Jack decided not to stop when he was flagged down,' says Ali. 'The border police caught up with us when we were crossing this bridge over a river. One of them grabbed Jack's passport and when he opened it a wrap of coke fell out. The cop held it up and was about to ask what it was when, to our amazement, Jack grabbed it from between the cop's fingers and flung it over the side of the bridge.

'We were all pissing ourselves laughing but the cops didn't see the funny side. They dragged Jack from the car and started beating him with their batons.

'All of us were being quite mouthy until one of the police got a teargas canister and held it inches from my face, as if to say: "Another dicky bird and you'll be gassed." We were then taken down to the station and strip-searched while a cop went to look for the wrap by the river bank. He found it, soaking wet, and Jack claimed that it wasn't his. Then, as if from nowhere, they produced a 25-guilder bag of hash – one of those little bags you buy in Amsterdam – fined us 5,000 francs and let us go.

'Even then Jack started shouting, "I'm not paying that! That's outrageous!" But there was a reason. We later found out that he had been deliberately playing up to distract attention from the fact that there were kilos of coke strapped underneath the chassis of the car.'

Our travels have also taught us that the potential for danger exists in those parts of the world where the value placed on life is so low.

We've been held to ransom and 'fined' for buying coke by corrupt cops in Brazil. Once we had a gun pulled on us in New York and Norman saved the day by puffing out his chest and walking onto the gun. The guy backed off. Norman did the same another time in Chicago, late at night in a shop. We only dropped into the store to buy some cigarettes when this huge bloke pulled a gun and started waving it around. Norman walked over to him and said, 'You've got one shot. Then I'm going to stick it up your arse and pull the trigger.'

The guy went, 'Hey I was only joking! You limeys sure are crazy!'

Norman once got into a spot of hot water in the company of one of our legendary crew members, Gabby, who handled security for us at the time. Gabby has a 56-inch chest and was once bodyguard for Eddie Futrell, the godfather of Birmingham nightlife in the 70s.

There are many legends attached to Gabby – going back to the Krays – but one of the most notable relates to a night when he went out with Norman to a longshoreman's bar on the waterfront in New York. Norman was, shall we say, behaving a bit boisterously, and Gabby realised that he might have to persuade him out of the premises. Before he could, the barman came around the bar clutching a baseball bat and swung it at Norman. Gabby held his arm up and the bat shattered to smithereens, with the barman left holding the handle. Gabby said, 'There's no need for that, is there?'

The barman shook his head meekly. 'No. . .'

Gabby got Norman outside and one of the blokes started goading him through the door window, giving it all that on the other side of the glass. Before Gabby could intervene, Norman went *WHAAP!* and knocked him clean out, straight through the pane.

The next morning Gabby showed us his arm. Sure there was some bruising, but for any lesser mortal a blow like that would have broken bones and done some severe damage.

At the other end of the scale, because we have played places that no other bands will dare visit, we have received the full-on treatment in certain countries. During the South American tour promoting *Promises and Lies* in the early 90s we would arrive in cities in Colombia, Chile, Brazil, Argentina, wherever, in our own plane with Virgin Records and UB40 emblazoned down the side. We'd be met by a military police escort, complete with armoured cars, which would drive us to the venue without regard for traffic lights or pedestrian safety.

Once in Colombia, civil unrest was so rife that we were locked in our hotel rooms for our own safety, and the first time we played Sri Lanka it was for a so-called 'peace celebration' when a delicate truce had been negotiated between the government and the Tamil rebels. All had been quiet for a year after two decades of savage bomb attacks in the capital, Colombo. We were told we couldn't play the arena we had been booked into because there had been a thunderstorm and it was waterlogged, so we would have to transfer to the R. Premadasa International Cricket Stadium.

The stage was set up on one side of the ground and the audience was placed a hundred yards away in the opposite stand. When we turned up to play we were told that the Sri Lankan Cricket Board had ruled that none of the audience members would be allowed onto the pitch. 'I told the promoter, "You do realise we're a dance band? It's no good having the crowd right over there. The atmosphere will be ruined",' says Robin. 'The guy said, "We can't do that. There's a match against New Zealand next week!"'

They put some groundsheets down to allow a couple of hundred people in front of the stage but that wasn't good enough, and we refused to go on.

The next thing we knew the Sri Lankan minister of sport and the minister for the interior were involved, begging us to perform.

To refuse would have been a slap in the face to the fans. It was a fait accompli, so grudgingly we went on and Lanval, one of our management team, went around the pitch screaming at the police officers to let the kids on. By the time we finished the show there was a decent number in front of the stage, though yet again we had been placed in a difficult position by ignorant promoters. These days we take it in our stride; it's the price you pay for sometimes playing in the back of beyond.

12

Labour of Love

After the *UB44* fiasco we knew we had to deliver, especially when the single 'I've Got Mine' barely scraped the Top 50, and a hastily released live album only got to number 44 – it had come out as a bit of a stopgap as the deal with CBS came to a close.

Rather than backing records like that, it was clear to us – if not to the more sceptical executives in the music business – that an album of covers of the greatest reggae songs of our youth would be massive. How could it fail? These were fantastic tunes that had been with us since we were kids. We knew 'Red Red Wine' was a dead cert hit even if nobody else did.

So our next album, which we called *Labour of Love*, was a way for us to answer the question which constantly plagued us in those days: 'Why do you play reggae?'

If an answer were needed, it was because these were the songs of the late 60s and early 70s that had put us all on the path to making music.

But whenever we had suggested a covers album to CBS or anyone else in the music biz the reaction had been: 'Covers of old reggae hits? Don't be stupid! UB40 are a dole-queue band. You can't do a cabaret album!'

The wisdom in the industry was that we would destroy our following, who, it was claimed, were into the political nature of the band. We strongly believed that our fans were into the music just as much as, if not more than, the politics. Richard Branson's deal with us was based again on the promise that nobody from the record company would interfere with our music, so we set about making the record at our new studio, on the east side of Birmingham (where we still are to this day).

We had been based in offices on Albert Street in the centre of town but it became clear that we needed space for our own studio as well and our business manager, Paul Davies, suggested the disused slaughterhouse as a possible location. It was cheap and needed a lot of work, but was ideally situated, away from the bustle of the city centre.

We spent months getting the place shipshape, scrubbing dried blood off the walls. Although pretty basic, by the late summer of 1982 it was possible to start recording there.

'It was great to have our own studio at last,' says Robin. 'Not least because there were less casualties among the engineers! When we had previously recorded at other studios we drove them mad, because the keyboard player or whoever would turn up at 4 a.m. expecting to get some work done. The engineers would end up working twenty-hour days trying to satisfy each of us, and would eventually crack up.'

In keeping with its previous incarnation, we named the studio the Abattoir. There was a tin shed where our offices are now and in there we installed our own recording equipment and engineer Howard Gray, who had worked on mixing *UB44*.

Howard lasted the course and was brilliant to work with, though even he went nuts at one point. 'I remember him losing it and getting up and walking across the brand-new desk one day, stamping on the faders and crushing half a dozen channels,' says

Robin. 'I can't blame him because engineers are like everybody else. They can only take so much pressure from all eight of us.'

Produced collectively with Ray 'Pablo' Falconer, the sessions for *Labour of Love* were a joy because we knew every song back to front. Robin compiled a list of tunes from 1969 to 1972 and then the rest of the band went through them, adding and subtracting till we got exactly the right mix.

One of the big bonuses of making the record was working on the sessions with one of our heroes: the legendary JA keyboard player Jackie Mittoo. We'd say to him, 'We're doing this song,' and Jackie would say, 'Oh, I played on that.' Then we'd mention another song and he'd go, 'A'me dat too.'

'After Jackie left we discovered the huge pile of empty whisky bottles he had left outside the shed. God knows how he laid down all that amazing keyboard stuff having swallowed that lot!' says Robin. A sign of his genius maybe. He'd be knocking them back and then suddenly say, 'Spin it.' The tape would roll and Jackie would just turn it on. If he ever fucked up – and that was rare – Jackie would say, 'Take it back,' and we'd rewind and he'd drop in something perfect. Jackie bought a touch of magic to that album.

Labour of Love was recorded over a six-month period, and within a couple of weeks of its release date in the summer of 1983, in typical UBs style, we ran out of money. Although the royalties were coming in, we had spent a lot on the Abattoir, and the relative flop of *UB44* – not to mention the hologram debacle – had placed us in dire straits. All the while we wished we were in Dire Straits!

There was another factor, which we discovered to our substantial cost many years later. It's our understanding that Paul Davies had failed to register UB40 with the major music industry societies around the world who collect performance money for songs played live and on the radio and TV, so a crucial income stream was cut off for a very long time.

'Red Red Wine' was released as the first single from the album and we all had our fingers crossed; there was just enough money in the pot to pay the wages at the Abattoir for another couple of weeks. Unless a miracle occurred everything was about to go kaput.

Virgin were fully behind us, though, constantly telling us we had a great record on our hands. And by the time the news came through that 'Red Red Wine' had gone to number one, we were down in London engaged in press and promotional interviews.

The excited staff at the record company expected us to start jumping in the air but our reaction was: 'About time too.' We've always had a touch of arrogance because we truly believe that any success that comes to us is deserved, just as much as any failure is.

Labour of Love went on to sell ten million copies and 'Red Red Wine' stayed at number one for three weeks and was then followed by three other big hits from the album, 'Please Don't Make Me Cry', 'Many Rivers to Cross' and 'Cherry Oh Baby'.

In the video for 'Cherry Oh Baby', Brian egged on the director Bernard Rose to make Ali snog Mickey's girlfriend, Bernadette. All the while Mickey was frowning out of shot. The footage became part of a film we put together (also called *Labour of Love*) which helped Brian carve a reputation as one of the UK's leading video directors of the 80s.

What with all the hits, the pressure was then on from Virgin to produce *Labour of Love Volume* II, but we just weren't interested for the time being. When the money from *Labour of Love* came in, we ploughed it into moving the studio out of the shed into the basement of the Abattoir, and kitted it out with some decent recording technology, complete with two built-from-scratch 24-track studios.

We insisted on handling everything ourselves, from writing, record production, studio management and videos to our music publisher New Claims, DEP Records and merchandising. Our inexperience in most, if not all, of these areas was to take its toll on our future financial security. It was to be years before we discovered the extent of the business ineptitude undermining us.

'We had earned a fortune but everything we made was just paid back into those loss-making companies,' says Robin. 'The success of *Labour of Love* in 1983 provided enough funds to get everything working again but it took us five years to get everything on an even keel.'

We also signed Jamaican artists Mikey Dread and Winston Reedy to DEP and they set about working on their own albums. Meantime we ploughed £60,000 into Echobass, the group set up by our old mate Jimmy Lynn. Echobass's album was recorded and mixed twice yet never saw the light of day. Another victim of the sometimes tortuous process of producing records.

Since Branson had granted us creative control, we could tell Virgin that we would make another *Labour of Love* when we thought the time was right without any repercussions.

The way we chose to follow it up was with the album *Geffery Morgan*, the ridiculous title of which came from a piece of graffiti Brian and Ali thought was hilarious. Written on a brick wall was the slogan: 'Geffery Morgan loves white girls. . .'

So, in their wisdom, Brian and Ali said that should be the full title of the album. Virgin begged us to take '. . . loves white girls . . .' off the cover, so the photograph is on the inside. And of course the album was a total flop because the rule is: if the record company isn't behind the album, then it isn't going to fly. *Geffery Morgan* probably sold about a million copies around the world, but in our book that's not good.

The first single was 'If It Happens Again', which had originally been 'Bouncing Around', one of the first songs Ali, Earl and Jimmy played that fateful day in 1978 when Robin decided to join the band.

'If It Happens Again' was a brilliant single and a great follow-up to the *Labour of Love* stuff, cracking the Top Ten and helped by the fact that we were automatically put on radio playlists because of our recent successes.

But we still had a problem: the single appeared on an album with one of the stupidest titles in pop history! The two follow-ups were complete flops – 'Riddle Me' only reached number 59 while 'I'm Not Fooled So Easily' scraped by at number 79.

Although we had scored major recent success with *Labour of Love*, the money we received from that was blown not only on setting DEP up but also on maintaining our increasingly expensive lifestyles. Cocaine was still the drug *du jour* with many band members, and tensions started to come to the fore.

13

'I Got You Babe'

Although it was Ali's duet with Chrissie Hynde on 'I Got You Babe' which helped dig UB40 out of the hole by hitting the number-one spot in the summer of 1985, there has always been a bit of argy-bargy about whose idea it was to cover the Sonny & Cher classic in the first place.

'The first single I ever had – bought for me by Mom – was the original by Sonny & Cher,' says Ali. 'Chrissie has always said it was her idea that we should do it, but I've been singing that song since I was five years old.'

It's true that Chrissie was always insistent we should make a record together whenever we bumped into each other on the road. 'With your voices and my looks we could go far,' she'd wise-crack in that accent of hers.

So, having decided on the collaboration, we got back to Birmingham and assembled the backing track together in the studio. She then came up to The Abattoir – which would eventually take on the name DEP as well – and put down her vocal.

'Producing Chrissie was a breeze because she is totally humble about her work,' says Robin. 'She'd say, "Tell me what vocal you like, and tell me if I'm crap." Armed with that, it was an easy job to coax a great performance out of her. She's as good as gold and a total pro.'

The video for 'I Got You Babe' was shot during a soundcheck at Jones Beach, New York by the director Jonathan Demme, who had already made a name for himself with the Talking Heads movie *Stop Making Sense* and would go on to become Hollywood A-list with films like *Something Wild* and *Philadelphia*. Somehow, Demme even managed to get a cameo appearance by his 71-year-old mother into the plot!

Whatever, the simplicity of the video and the quality of the song propelled us back to the number-one slot.

Two years later we got back together with Chrissie and recorded 'Breakfast in Bed', which went to number 6 in the charts in June 1988. 'Breakfast in Bed' was similar to the 'Red, Red Wine' situation, since we only knew the reggae version by Lorna Bennett while Chrissie – being older than us – was familiar with the song from Dusty Springfield's album *Dusty in Memphis*.

This time the video for 'Breakfast in Bed' was filmed in Birmingham, and Ali is featured as a conman pretending to be a vicar who pops round to Chrissie's house. This came from a never-completed film called *Dance with the Devil* which also starred Keith Allen and Robert Palmer amongst others.

Since 'Breakfast in Bed' we've often talked about working with Chrissie again. She is just as keen as us, so who knows? If the right song comes along, we'd be bang up for it.

We knew that there was a perception building that the only hits we could achieve were cover versions, and some members of the band were even affected by the adverse criticism, but we brothers weren't – and still aren't – bothered in the slightest.

'In fact, I usually agree with criticism if a valid point is being made,' says Ali. 'My voice doesn't come in for much flak anyway.'

Back in 1985, the success of 'I Got You Babe' soon saw us on the upward curve again, although the year was marred by the end of Robin's relationship with his girlfriend of five years, Nicky. 'We didn't have two pennies to rub together when I first knew her, but was a successful pop star by the time we split up,' he says. 'Nicky was a darling, a lovely girl, but we just drifted apart over the years as our lives took different paths. It was nobody's fault, and there was nobody else involved.'

Around this time Robin opened his own club, UB's, with our brother Duncan. 'It was rammed every Thursday, Friday and Saturday night,' says Robin. 'I had my own table, raised on a platform in the corner. If other bands were in town they'd come down for a drink. We had reggae some nights, and to reflect Dunc's musical interests, it also had a Sunday lunchtime folk club.'

Ali didn't frequent UB's. 'I was still living in Balsall Heath and drinking a lot, but in the small back-street pubs near our studio,' he says. 'That was the way I dealt with fame, by going to places where nobody really cared who I was. I wouldn't go to UB's, not because I didn't like it, but because people would treat me like a pop star, and that has always made me feel very uncomfortable. Still does.

'Once I was mobbed in Tesco's and stuck in there for about an hour and a half. I couldn't go back for about four years, even though it was my local supermarket. It was a nightmare being surrounded by a mass of people, most of whom didn't know who I was, just that I was famous. Really horrible.'

Robin, on the other hand, enjoyed the experience. 'I was living the life and driving around in a Ferrari, until the front end was bashed in by a drunk in a Jag,' he grins. 'He pulled out in front of me and BOSH! That was that.'

To this day we still receive differing reactions from the public. 'Ali is gregarious, a natural smiler, so he is approached a lot more than me,' says Robin. 'I have a reputation for being a miserable bastard – which I'm not by the way, but it comes in dead handy sometimes! When I'm walking through town I adopt an attitude which sends out the vibe: "Don't bother me." It is lovely when people say hi or want to shake your hand, don't get me wrong. I never refuse an autograph and I'm never rude but sometimes people will take liberties. I've only refused on half a dozen occasions in twenty-five years, usually because I'm trying to have a private meal with a friend and a fan wants to interrupt.

'But I look back on UB's fondly, not just because it was a great club, but also because I was on my own turf and could enjoy all the benefits of being a pop star without being pestered.'

UB's wasn't ideally situated for a reggae club: it took up the basement of the headquarters of West Midlands Serious Crime Squad, the cops who put the Birmingham Six away and were eventually disbanded when their cover was blown. During the 70s and 80s they had the worst reputation for locking people up just for having thick lips and curly hair. Initially there weren't any objections when UB's opened, but the attitude changed as soon as reggae started booming out of there.

'For the first eight months UB's was absolutely packed, with queues around the corner. Then a very high-ranking police officer told us, "Close down and reopen as a nice white wine bar and you'll have no trouble from us,"' says Robin. 'Duncan's reaction was straightforward enough: "Fuck off. We're breaking no laws. And it's not a black club; everyone is welcome here." The officer said: "I don't care whether it takes me six months or a couple of years, but I will close you down." We laughed it off at the time but soon I was away with the band on a six-week tour and the night I got back I went down to UB's and there were a dozen people there at most. The cops had been coming in every night, stopping the music, turning the lights on and searching customers. If I'd had any business sense at all I would have closed UB's there and then but I was determined, and tried to revive trade over the next year. But it never recovered and eventually I was forced to shut up shop.'

Robin met his next girlfriend, Sindy, at UB's and well recalls the reaction to them being a mixed couple. 'We used to go to black venues to watch reggae artists and I'd hear comments made to her about her being with a white man,' he says. 'She'd always say to me: "Take no notice, they're just wankers."'

'When I look back I realise that Sindy was far too young and far too beautiful and I was far too old and far too wealthy. But hindsight is 20/20 isn't it? I only realised much later how different we were.'

Later in 1985, 'Don't Break My Heart' went Top Three. Within a few years we found out the truth in the old music biz saying: where there's a hit there's a writ.

'This mate of mine from Balsall Heath, Javid Khan, came to me with eight lines of lyrics scrawled on a beer mat,' says Ali. 'There was some great stuff there but none of it rhymed and it was a bit of a mess, so I completely rewrote them and came up with a song.'

The original idea was that Javid would sing it, but he couldn't handle the vocal, so we paid him £10,000 and I recorded this wicked song myself. It was only after the single came out that we discovered the original lines Javid had brought to me weren't actually his, but taken from a poem written by an English teacher he knew.

She brought a case against us for breach of copyright, and in 1995 it finally reached court, where she was awarded £50,000 in back royalties while the court costs were another £250,000.

In his summing up, the judge said he found us to be honest and forthright in our statements. He made sure that no blame could be attached to us, but awarded her an equal share of the songwriting with the eight of us. So she received a ninth, which was still a sizeable amount of money because it was such a big hit. Javid had moved back to Pakistan by this time, but came to England for the case and was brilliant. He looked like Omar Sharif with those prunes-and-custard eyes, saying, 'How could you call me liar?'

The scale of the success of 'Don't Break My Heart' propelled us back into the studio to put together the dub album *Baggariddim*. This was followed by the EP *Little Baggariddim* and, in the following year, the album *Rat in the Kitchen*, which included the Top Twenty hits 'Rat in Mi Kitchen' and 'Sing Our Own Song'.

Then, at the end of 1987, just as we were celebrating the fact that *The Best of UB40 – Volume I* had reached the number-three spot, tragedy struck. One night, while driving home with his brother – and our engineer – Ray, Earl's Volvo lost control and hit a wall. Ray was killed outright and Earl was charged with having twice the legal limit of alcohol in his bloodstream.

It was horrendous. We got the call from the office and all sat around stunned at the news. Ray was family, blood. He was all set to be involved in engineering our next album, but more than anything, he made a major contribution to UB40 live.

Ray was very creative and would be doing all sorts of weird, crazy and wonderful things, dubbing while we played as well as mixing the overall sound. He was a bit like Scratch, the mad sonic doctor full of off-the-wall ideas. Nobody – not even the most technically gifted sound people – has ever been able to recreate what Ray did for us live.

We miss him to this day.

14

On the Road

1988 was to prove the turning point in our lives and the career of UB40, a year of exhilarating highs and extremely depressing lows.

That spring we completed a new album – simply entitled *UB40* – and by April we were once again looking for a manager after splitting with Ken Freedman, who had handled our affairs for a few years by then.

Ken, who entered our lives after our brother Dave gave up the management reins, was from Los Angeles and had started in the business in the traditional American way, as a band-booker at college. By the time we met him, he was working in the recording industry and approached us saying he could help us achieve the heights of success in the States.

'I remember Ken taking us to Rodeo Drive and buying us all fancy shirts,' says Ali. 'Then we went back to his house, an amazing place in Beverly Hills. But when it came to it, we had to move on because UB40 wasn't making headway. And it turned out we had to tell him twice for the message to sink in. He only really got the idea we were serious the second time around! It cracked me up, and Ken said in that American accent of his, "Ali, I know you're not laughing at me but laughing with me . . .'"

When we started looking for a replacement, Ali mentioned that he had admired the way Robert Palmer was portrayed in the media. We always seemed to have a crap time at the hands of the press, who depicted us as uncool and bland or, worse, dour. Robert, on the other hand, was forever in *Vogue* and other wickedly stylish magazines, and always seemed to be in the right place at the right time, with great records and sharp clothes.

As it happened, around this time Brian was running his video production company in London and met Robert, who made the introduction to his manager, this guy called Dave Harper.

Through Brian we set up a meeting in London with Dave. He turned up looking slick and groovy – like Robert Palmer in fact! – and talked such a good talk we opted to go with him. One of the things that won us over was that he admitted he was very flattered that we had approached him in the first place.

Dave came along at exactly the right time, and he asked us a very basic question, which was to have a major impact on the next six years of our lives and beyond.

'Why don't you tour for more than six weeks at a time?' he demanded. Before we could answer, Dave told us, 'The only way you'll make serious money is by getting on the road and seriously promoting your records.' Every manager we had ever had had told us the same thing, but up until then we'd been wrapped up in our own worlds, marrying, settling into new houses and raising families. None of us had wanted to leave home for too long and we simply didn't have the ambition. 'My son was fourteen months old in 1988,' says Robin. 'I had a nice house in Moseley with Sindy, while Ali was in Balsall Heath with Bernie, Ali Jr and Max – who were tiny kids then – and his daughter Kibibi on the way.'

Robin says that the global approach to touring was also anathema to the rest of the band. 'Once in the mid-80s we played with

Sting,' he adds. 'Sting was moaning on, "Four years I've been doing this!" We couldn't comprehend that. "Four years on the road — is he fucking mental?"'

We'd started off with this plan to release an album every year with a dub album in between, but that had fallen by the wayside after *Present Arms in Dub* and *Little Baggariddim*. Since then we had locked ourselves into a routine of promoting every UB40 album release with tours which were split up into a few weeks at a time.

The cost of putting UB40 on the road for relatively short stretches meant that we consistently lost money. All the advances and income from record sales were swallowed up by supporting the eight of us and the infrastructure at DEP. Anything that was left over went towards the cost of playing live. It was a crazy situation.

Dave's point was that once the UB40 juggernaut was rolling it should be kept on the road, so that the more performances we gave the steadier the income to offset those hefty tour costs.

Looking back, he hit us with this philosophy at the right time. We had become too settled in our ways, and now that our kids were growing up — and the school fees were really kicking in! — the time was right to go out and play for protracted periods and earn some serious dosh.

'Dave said what we wanted to hear,' says Robin. 'We knew it was the right thing to do. Going out for two-to-six-week stints with as many as forty-two of us to feed, bed and board was madness. But we were all in denial about it, so when Dave chirped up it was a bit of a relief. He didn't have to convince us.'

With the new album ready to go, Dave sorted us out a full-on world tour. At first the schedule looked like it was going to take us away from home for several months but as events played out, we ended up with the band being away from home for nearly two-and-a-half years. Not only did we go to Australia, New Zealand, Japan, Brazil and Argentina, but we also went to places we'd never played before, from Abu Dhabi and Dubai to Israel and Hungary.

Our partners and kids were already used to us going away a lot, but up until then we had been coming home a lot as well. This time it was different, and the stress gradually began to reveal itself over the ensuing years.

'I can't pinpoint exactly when I became a stranger in my own home because everything was such a blur, but by the end of that period, that was what had happened to me,' says Robin. 'I am sure that if I hadn't gone on the road all that time, my relationship with Sindy wouldn't have broken down in the way that it did. While I was away she started to live a different life, and alcohol and cocaine became part of that.'

With that first big tour, Dave proved himself to be an astute businessman, though his behaviour often verged on the outrageous, insulting record company heads and generally behaving like a rock star rather than a band manager.

On 11 July 1988 we played the concert at Wembley Stadium to accelerate the release of Nelson Mandela from jail. Apart from Whitney Houston's entourage insisting that her backdrop – for her sponsor Coca-Cola – was draped over the Free Nelson Mandela banner, it was quite a day. Beamed around the world to millions of people, we played a set which included 'Red Red Wine', still a crowd-pleaser even after five years, and soon to have an unexpected resurgence.

With just a week to go before the world tour was due to start, we received a heavy blow: Earl's court case stemming from the car crash the previous year reached Birmingham Crown Court. The judge sent him down for six months.

This was devastating. It had been harsh enough dealing with the fact that Ray was dead, but Earl's custodial sentence had been used to make an example of him – not because he was over the limit but because he was a member of a hit-making band.

We had never played a gig without the full line-up, but had

no choice but to leave our brother behind. After trying a few people out, we recruited a guy called Leroy Bushell on bass duties. He came along to rehearsals at DEP and had a few of our numbers already down. Leroy – who we christened 'Digbeth' – was shit-hot enough to grasp the whole set with ease, although he wasn't, and never could be, Earl.

In the end Earl was off the scene for the first four months of the tour, and the night he turned up he sat and watched the gig from the audience. He's the only member of the band who's ever been able to do that!

Meanwhile 'Red Red Wine' – which had topped the charts in countries all over the world, but only made number 24 in the States five years earlier – had started to take off again in America under the most freakish and accidental of circumstances.

A DJ in Phoenix, Arizona, had been programming his playlist using the station's random-select format. We were later told a Ziggy Marley track popped up, but he wasn't a fan of Bob's son. Then the computerised system disgorged a substitute suggestion, 'Red, Red Wine', which he recalled from the Nelson Mandela gig.

So the song went on the station playlist, and the reaction from listeners was such that he slotted it into the phone-in chart. The calls started flooding in. Once it got to number one on the Phoenix station's phone-in chart, other radio stations in Arizona began to add it. Then somebody from our US record company, A&M, called up and told us that they were re-releasing it as single because it was breaking out of Arizona and being played all over the States. Yee-hah!

As the American dates got under way, 'Red Red Wine' steadily climbed the *Billboard* Hot 100, and, on 15 October, the night we played a sold out Madison Square Gardens, we received the excited call from A&M: 'Red Red Wine' had gone to number one in the US. About time, we thought!

Labour of Love had also re-entered the American album chart, climbing to number 14, while *UB40* had gone to number 44. It was insane. Suddenly you couldn't move for UB40 and the media was all over us (well, for at least five minutes).

This was also a significant achievement for reggae music, which had made little headway in the mainstream music business in the States.

Sure, there had been one-hit wonders and crossover novelty tunes (the likes of 'Rivers of Babylon' by Boney M), but even Bob Marley had to be satisfied with his biggest hit, 'Could You be Loved', only reaching the mid-30s in the American R&B charts, and that was probably because he had toured with the Commodores and Stevie Wonder, who were huge.

Up until that point we'd been perceived as a bit of a novelty band ourselves. The radio programmers, concert promoters and venue operators of the US music industry didn't know where to place us, because we were a predominantly white band playing Caribbean music and there was no tradition of that in the States.

It was ridiculous. We'd get audience members coming up to us after shows and asking whether we'd just been on holiday in Jamaica, as if that was the reason we played reggae.

We had been slogging around the 'sheds' – seated venues with fields for picnickers with crowd capacities around 12,000 – and had carved out a live reputation to rival other British bands then making the moves in the States, such as Depeche Mode, U2 and Simple Minds. All three of them had been catapulted into another league by scoring US number ones and now we looked like following them.

'Even though we were still treated as a novelty by the record company, "Red Red Wine" made such a difference to our careers as live performers in the States,' says Robin. 'Having played the sheds we thought we could move up to the stadiums, but somehow that success didn't translate for us in the same way as it did for some other bands.'

Since 'Red Red Wine' had reignited interest in the *Labour of*

Love album, the decision was made to come up with a second volume of reggae covers, recording of which we squeezed in between live dates in the South of France, Italy and even Hawaii.

We undertook some really gruelling tours. After the summer sheds we'd do six weeks of college dates, often when the colleges were closed. It was pretty desperate for a band that had just had a number-one hit.

The college tours that we played drew mainly white audiences made up of students, but, wherever there were concentrations of black and other ethnic minorities – say, in Miami – we also attracted blacks and Latinos. Even in the deepest south the audiences would be mixed. One night in Austin, Texas things got very hairy. We were playing this bar which was absolutely heaving, with ten-gallon hats being thrown into the air and shouts of 'Yee-ha!'

Just before the show some local kids had given us a leaflet about anti-Klan activity in the area; it claimed that the KKK had been garotting black schoolchildren.

When we got to 'One in Ten', Astro went into this speech: 'Stop, stop, crowd of people, hear me now!' Holding up the leaflet he said, 'Listen! Are you gonna let this happen to the children in your neighbourhood?!'

We all expected them to roar, 'Nooo!'

But you could have heard a mouse fart. Old and young, black or white, none of them wanted to know.

The reason? The people in that multicultural audience had to live side by side with one another. It was OK for us Limey pop stars to ride into town and get all worked up about it, but this was an issue they faced on a daily basis. That underlined to us that we should never become embroiled in local politics. We're out of there the next day leaving the communities to deal with the consequences of our interfering.

The year-long tour of 1988-9 sparked the most intensive work period in the band's history: we barely drew breath as Dave Harper hammered home to us the advantages of undertaking year-out tours, one after another. Just to stay on the road – and avoid the cost of breaking everything down and then having to set up again – we'd be out on a highway in some northerly state in the snow and ice, packing in the crowds, making merry after the gig and then leaving town for the next night's performance.

We all had our different coping mechanisms on the road. One of Robin's was to start using marijuana more. 'That was when I started buying it for the first time, rather than having a couple of drags off other people,' he says. 'Up until then I'd have a draw at a party or in somebody's room, but weed relaxes me and evens me out, gets rid of my rage. And a lot of that was building inside me because of our punishing schedule. If I feel like killing somebody I have a joint and suddenly I don't any more.'

In many ways the constant touring had a horrible impact on our personalities, because you have to bottle up so much. There's no point in losing it, because the job is all about hanging around for things to be set up. You just have to be as patient as possible. As Rolling Stones drummer Charlie Watts has said, playing live in a band is waiting around for twenty-three hours every day.

During that period we released three top-selling albums, scored numerous hits including three number ones and toured the world.

For four and a half out of those six years, we were at home for only very short breaks. 'It just seemed to go on and on,' says Robin. 'The last thing I wanted to do was get into coke so I chose weed, because it made me mellow.'

As for Ali, his drinking and drugging reached new heights. 'I truly believe I have never been the same since the first 28-hour trip we took to Australia in the early 80s,' says Ali. 'Seriously, I have never had my feet back on the ground since that flight. Before I started all this, I felt "normal". But I remember clearly getting off that flight with my first real case of jet lag and I've never been the same since. Then I helped "not being normal" along with sustained alcohol and cocaine abuse for decades.'

Robin was in despair at Ali's condition. 'I spent years confronting him but he was deeply in denial. By a certain point on tour he would be reasonably sober at the beginning of every show and rat-arsed by the end. I was just not interested in being on the road with him. Every gig would be so tense, because I'd be waiting for him to make a mistake.

It was a horrible experience watching Ali become an alcoholic, especially since it runs in the family. I'd think, oh God, here we go again. . .'

15

Promises and Lies

In June 1989 we arrived home exhausted, having spent a total of just six weeks in the UK to take advantage of the so-called 'year-out' tax benefits.

Having breathed a collective sigh of relief, we stayed put for the rest of the year only to find that, due to a financial miscalculation, we'd actually have to spend the following two years on the road. Apparently a larger-than-expected tax bill had come in based on our earnings in 1988 and it had to be paid.

In effect we became tax exiles, roaming the globe for four more years as our hard work bred more and more success and income. 'Compared to everyone else we knew, we were loaded,' confirms Robin. 'I had a bar and a Ferrari while my friends who I'd known since Leyland were still working there.'

So, in 1990 we all upped sticks again and hauled ass onto the road, initially to promote that year's release of *Labour of Love II*, which gave us three Top Ten hits in America alone, as well as our version of 'I'll Be Your Baby Tonight' with the late great Robert Palmer.

We had first met Robert years earlier, in 1981 when, at *Top of the Pops*, he came over to Ali and said, 'I love that ska thing you do,' pronouncing 'ska' really short and clipped in his Yorkshire accent. The hook-up on 'I'll Be Your Baby Tonight' came about because of the managerial links with Dave Harper. By that time we'd played live together, with Robert sometimes opening for us.

For almost all of the band and crew, the constant touring wreaked havoc on our personal lives, particularly when it came to sustaining marriages and relationships. In those circumstances, you end up living different lives and become different people. The irony is that, although this was our most successful period financially and in terms of hits, it was also the most destructive. We would try and make up for our absences by spending a fortune flying our missuses and kids out to join us whenever we had a chance; forty people on a week-long holiday in Jamaica or Hawaii, that sort of thing. There we'd be, taking over a posh hotel or a five-star resort with thirty-odd kids running riot, all of them with no fear of authority.

'We spent ridiculous amounts of money on holidays,' says Ali. 'We'd set up cottages on the beach in the Caribbean. Once eleven of us went on a week-long safari holiday in Africa at the cost of £1,000 per day per person. Add up those figures – £77,000 for a holiday is a bit much!'

Although our lifestyles changed, with bigger houses and better cars and more expensive schools, the sad fact was that we grew apart from our partners. All of the common interests you share come undone in these situations and the one left behind has to create their own social circle and a new life for themselves.

'On the road we were living the life of Reilly, and then coming home as strangers,' says Robin. 'It was difficult to take on board the fact that their lives had been progressing while you had been in suspended animation in a cocoon of gigs, hotel rooms, parties and tour buses.

'There were plenty of times when I would arrive home and question what I was doing there, I was that unhappy. Sometimes it came down to the most trivial things. I'd switch on the TV and be told by the rest of the family that they were in the habit of watching this or that programme on the other side.

'In 1988 my son Matt was fourteen months old. The next time I came back for a longish break in 1991 he was three and a half. Of course I'd seen him every so often, but I missed out on a crucial stage in his growing up.'

Robin now sees that his relationship with Sindy was over by 1990, but the couple stayed together, at first because their daughter Amy was born the following year. 'I kept on asking Sindy to leave because I couldn't stand her drinking, but everything changed when she became pregnant,' he says. 'Sindy did stop while she was pregnant and when Amy arrived. But as soon as I was back on the road she went back to it. During that period I would only be at home for periods of a few weeks at a time, so things began to get out of control. I wasn't around to help her and she couldn't cope on her own.'

The grind continued. In 1992 we recorded *Promises and Lies*, and that took us back on the merry-go-round for another fifteen months, with our fortunes bolstered by the single 'I Can't Help Falling in Love with You', which spent seven weeks at number one in the States after it was used in the Sharon Stone movie *Sliver*. This put us on a sales level we thought we'd never attain; soon *Promises and Lies* was rocketing up the charts and we were scoring hits all over and selling ten million albums in twelve months.

'One day I arrived home in 1994 not only to an empty marriage but also to find Matt was a seven-year-old and Amy was three,' says Robin. 'It was no surprise to me that Sindy and I grew apart but it was devastating to have missed the important years of my children growing up. Once that's gone you can't get it back.'

In a way we, as brothers, went through the same experience during our own childhoods. As we've already said our own dad was away on the road for significant amounts of time. 'I guess our kids learnt to cope with that, just as we learnt to cope,' says Robin. 'Our children have dealt with the fact that we are high-profile people. The difference is our dad was a folksinger, whereas our kids love the fact that we are in UB40 and come to all the gigs and enjoy the perks of their fathers being in a band.'

During those years, when we got home it would only take the band and crew a week or so before we gravitated towards each other again. There was a pattern. Three, four, seven days at most of being with our women and kids and we'd start socialising again, always in the same places: the Town Cryer, the Oddfellows, Billy's Bar. You'd walk into the pub and every fucker would be in there, going: 'Wa-hey!'

We headed for each others' company because it was difficult to communicate with even your oldest friends. They'd ask, 'What have you been up to then?' You'd been around the world, playing every single country imaginable, and they were in the same place you'd left them a year previously.

'We'd be in a normal pub, trying to be "normal", but everything we talked about was alien to outsiders,' says Ali. 'Either they'd think you were showing off when you talked about the adventures and exotic locations, or think you were lying or gone mad!'

Some of the band cracked up. One in particular, who shall remain nameless, was really balanced for the first twelve months of the *Promises and Lies* tour, but when it was extended by another three months he just couldn't take it and started necking Es and behaving like a lunatic. Another, who had always been able to drink for days and not show a bother on him, collapsed through nervous exhaustion. Ali was still out there boozing and drugging as well, and he wasn't to reach his personal crossroads for another four years.

The consumption of alcohol and drugs on that tour was on the same kind of level as legendary hellraisers like Motörhead. People would come from different parts of showbusiness – we're not going to name them but, believe us, world-class, famous piss-heads – to try and drink Brian or Ali under the table and they'd leave them lying on their backs.

'The danger is that it becomes a lifestyle, and I realised that I had to make a conscious decision not to go with the flow, or I'd be eaten up by it,' says Robin by way of explanation of his strategy for surviving the pressures of the road. 'That's why I've always kept myself to myself. I withdraw to my room and watch movies. I'll have some wine and a smoke, but always make sure I get my sleep so that I can do my job. That's when you appear unsociable and unfriendly, when in fact you're fucked and just want to get to bed.'

16

High Times

We have always been publicly vocal about weed-smoking because we believe smoking it is a human right.

It's because we are so passionate about that right that we have supported the various legalisation campaigns over the years. We love our weed; it is a way of life and we understand the subject well. Let's face it, we've done enough research!

There are two basic types of weed because there are two types of its chemical constituent, THC – tetrahydrocannabinol – which release the endorphins in your brain.

Both have their uses. One type is more of a downer (skunk is a prime example); the other is irie, which makes you feel up and lively, like sensi. We totally reject the argument that marijuana is the entry level for drug abuse. Look at the statistics: the number of people who regularly use it in this country must run into the tens of millions, while the number of heroin users is under 500,000.

The criminality attached to marijuana is a disgrace and the government is basically a giant tobacco dealer, making £40m a year out of VAT on cigarettes, which are far more harmful to the nation's health and a far bigger drain on our medical resources.

'It's outrageous. The whole issue is steeped in hypocrisy,' says Robin. 'Where's the justification for legislation in favour of, and taxation from, tobacco and alcohol yet marijuana is criminalised? Where's the morals, the logic, the law?'

A few years back we recorded our version of the Doors' 'Light My Fire' to point out what a prat we thought Ann Widdecombe had made of herself when she declared in the House of Commons that those found in possession of marijuana should be subjected to on-the-spot fines of up to £100.

We rigged up a giant caricature of Widdecombe – then shadow home secretary – with a spliff in one hand and put it on a 'ganjavan' which drove around London, in particular Parliament Square, playing the song.

Apparently she wasn't at all amused and threatened to sue us, though she never went through with it. Even Mr Nice – the legalisation campaigner Howard Marks – got involved, reflecting our opinion when he said, 'She's got no idea what's going on.'

Although we enjoyed making the point so publicly, nobody would touch the record after the furore broke, so in effect we shot ourselves in the foot commercially. The irony was that we had been asked to record the song for a Doors tribute album when the Stone Temple Pilots pulled out because of their singer's heroin problems.

Nobody can argue with our knowledge of weed, though. One of the first UB40 overseas interviews took place in Amsterdam. The journalist laid out ten spliffs and asked us to guess the content. We got six right – not bad for a bunch of wankers from Balsall Heath!

It was only natural that as well as all of the music magazines and national press, we would do several interviews with the underground magazine dedicated to the weed lifestyle, *High Times*, over the years.

One time we were all huddled with the *High Times* guys in a New York hotel meeting room close to the lobby, pronouncing on the subject of weed, pointing out that we weren't fourteen-year-olds but grown men making an informed choice, and that ganja smoking is a civil rights matter.

'Just as I went into a speech about my basic right to smoke weed in private as long as I don't harm anybody else, the door came crashing in,' recalls Ali. 'It was the cops. They stormed into the room after a tip-off from some hotel staff. I couldn't exactly back down so, as they took down our names, I was screaming, "See? This is exactly what I'm talking about!"'

Typical of us to actually be busted during a *High Times* interview! They let us off with a caution and went on their way.

Our most hilarious encounter with heavy-duty weed occurred when we played an open-air concert in Fréjus in the south of France while on tour with the Police.

We'd already played support for the Police, the first time in the summer of 1980 when they announced that their only British concert that year would be at Milton Keynes Bowl. We did a short, thirty-minute set and won over not only the Police but also a fair proportion of their audience.

We became good friends with the guys in the band and when it was decided that their Fréjus gig was to be shot for a movie called *Urgh! A Music War* – which stitched together performances by a lot of early 80s bands – they invited us along.

As we were waiting to go on and play, the heavens opened and it was announced that the gig would be cancelled. Police drummer Stewart Copeland always had prime weed on him, and sent a carrier bag of really strong poona bud round to our dressing rooms. He said, 'I'm really sorry to have made you stay an extra night for no reason, so hopefully this will make amends.'

With a night off ahead of us we all got stuck in and got hold-onto-the-furniture stoned. 'I'd never even bought an ounce of draw by that time but I certainly smoked an ounce that night!' says Robin.

Suddenly we heard the Police's manager Miles Copeland's voice: 'Do I see blue skies? Do I see blue skies? Yes I do!'

Oh no. The gig was on! And we were all out of our trees. Watch the sequence of the film when Sting introduces us. There's a delay after he shouts, 'It's UB40!' and then you see these eight stoned, paranoid individuals creep on stage and gingerly strap on their instruments.

We went through the first tune – '25%' – at Looney Tunes speed in a desperate attempt to get the whole thing over and done with.

'It was horrendous – I lost an entire sequence of our set,' admits Robin. 'In the film we look absolutely terrified. That is the only time in my life as a performer that I have come round during the middle of a song. The last thing I knew we were halfway through that first song, and the next thing I knew we were four songs later! Scary stuff!'

Our heaviest encounter with the law over weed occurred in the Seychelles in the summer of 1990. We'd just finished another world tour, having been all over, from Australia, New Zealand and Japan to the US, where we finished up a fifty-city tour with two massive gigs in San Diego.

When we were invited to the Seychelles by the Marxist president's son to play a festival there in late July, it seemed like the perfect opportunity to chill from the rigours of the road. We were told at the time that the president and the police chief were off the island, which we didn't think made any difference to our presence there.

At first we were made very welcome during our stay at the gorgeous Hotel Beau Vallon Bay in the islands' capital, Victoria. Then came a warning from the assistant chief of police, who was obviously out to make a name for himself in his boss's absence. We were informed that despite being official guests of the Seychelles government, if we were caught smoking there'd be trouble.

Nevertheless, the night of the gig we were given weed by some cops, and the promoter threw a party at which everyone openly smoked draw. One sergeant did tell us to watch our step, though, since the assistant police chief seemed keen on feeling our collars.

There are some seriously impoverished people in the Seychelles, another fact we didn't really take on board. We found out for ourselves the night after the gig when we went up into the hills to hang out with the Seychellois, as they are known. A huge bonfire was lit, and, as fruitbats the size of dogs swooped about, the locals passed around flasks of the native moonshine, *kalu*, which tastes like armpit sweat but gets you seriously off your face. In a right old state we scored 1lb of malagash, the indigenous weed which is like Durban Poison, very seedy but upbeat and sparkly, very nice. Proper Marxist weed!

We took it back to the hotel where we were all staying, most of us paralytic.

'I was walking around the reception in the nude apparently,' says Ali. 'Somehow we managed to portion it all up and distributed it around the band members. Then I staggered off to bed.'

Robin had the presence of mind to hide his stash under a rock in a small courtyard outside his room, but at 8.30 a.m. on Monday 30 July the local police descended and raided the hotel, evidently acting on a tip-off, probably from one of the poor Seychellois hoping for some kind of kickback.

Of those in possession of the malagash, only us brothers escaped being hauled off to the local jail. 'Fortunately I had two rooms: one for my kids and the nanny, and the other for me and my missus,' says Ali. 'While the nanny's room was being searched my boy Ali, who was nine years old at the time, came into my bedroom and grabbed the bag of weed. It was still in my hand from where I had collapsed the previous night. Then he ran off up the beach with it in his bumbag.'

We only found out the next day that Gerry our sound engineer had been approached by a copper as he was leaving the hotel the night before. 'Gerry was advised to tell all of us to clear our rooms because a raid was definitely on,' says Robin. 'Unfortunately,

Gerry went out and got so pissed he couldn't remember what he was supposed to be warning us about!'

Jimmy, Brian, Astro and Earl and three crew members were jailed for a few days, pending further investigation. 'There was I, deep-sea fishing and happily smoking away while they lingered in the black hole,' says Ali. 'And I stayed there an extra week because I didn't want to leave until all the weed was finished!'

When the president of the Seychelles returned from a foreign trip the assistant police chief was promptly sacked but by that time the boys had been deported, which was preferable to the mandatory fifteen-year jail sentence. When they got back to England the press were all over them at the airport and it was covered by everyone from MTV News to Radio One.

The minister of arts and culture responsible for booking the band visited Robin and Ali twice with the government's abject apologies. 'The first time I wouldn't speak to him,' says Robin. 'The second time he sat on the floor while we were eating lunch, asking to make amends. We told him there was very little he could do to make up for throwing our bandmates, who were after all invited guests, out of the country!'

Over the years we have built up a worldwide network of connections as a result of our interest in weed. There isn't anywhere we can't obtain draw these days, a welcome change from the time when we had to take our own abroad with us and risk our careers and touring if we were discovered in possession. Being black and in UB40, Astro and Earl used to get a lot of attention, but we have all had our collars felt – most recently in Norway where they have zero tolerance, and Earl got pulled. They let him do the show and then he was taken off in handcuffs and put on a plane back home. He got dressed up in a Gucci suit so he'd look good in handcuffs.

'I've been busted many times, all over the world,' says Ali. 'Even in Canada, though I got away with it the time when I decided to hide my weed inside one of those plastic hotel shower caps. I had it in my ticket pocket and could tell from the customs officer's attitude that he was going to search me. First he went through my bag and then momentarily turned away, at which point I slipped the cap into the bag.

'As he was searching me, his mate bowled up and said to him, "Have you done this bag?" The first guy was busy frisking me and when he didn't answer, the other official unzipped one side. I could see the shower cap starting to inflate and mushroom out through the other zip like a jellyfish!

'Just as I thought the game was up, the first one said, "What are you doing? I've just done that bag!" and the second geezer walked away, leaving it alone. That was pretty close. I poked the shower cap back into the bag and strolled off.'

For Robin, the most annoying bust occurred in the south of France, and he still blames our drummer Jimmy to this day. 'Jimmy and I had stayed on for a few more days in Amsterdam when the rest of the band moved on to this lovely white château-hotel to start some recording not far from Nice,' he explains. 'We decided to bring down some ten-guilder bags of weed for the lads and got on the plane with an ounce and a half each stuffed down our trousers. Everything was fine, but while we were waiting at the baggage carousel this fucking customs guard walked in with a dog. I said to Jim, "Get away from me. If that dog sniffs either of us we don't want to be together, do we?" But it was too late. Jim actually started stroking the bloody thing, and of course the dog was all over him. They grabbed him and took me into a separate room with my hand luggage. I told them that the dog had been sniffing us because we had smoked marijuana in Amsterdam and there was obviously a residue in our clothing. I later found out Jimmy was in the next room telling them exactly the same story.

'They went through my bags and found nothing so I started to walk through to arrivals. Just as I spotted a policewoman with a machine gun standing on the other side of the final set of swing doors, it started: "M'sieur? M'sieur?" I ignored them until the woman barred my way with her gun. They walked me back into the search rooms and there was Jimmy, whimpering, "I didn't even know it was there! I forgot! I didn't mean to. . ." Apparently he'd forgotten that he'd left a wrap of coke in his bag!

'Their only response to both of us was: "Off wiz ze clothes!"

'I told them I didn't have anything like that and they repeated, "Off wiz ze clothes!"

'So I got the ounce and a half out of my trousers and said, "That's it. That's all I've got!" They asked me if I was sure and I pulled my sunglasses up to say yes. My eyes must have looked like smashed windscreens after our stay in Amsterdam. One went: "Les yeux! Les yeux!"

'And the other one went: "Off wiz ze clothes!"

'They strip-searched us, though they didn't go for the old "one up the bum, no harm done" routine, and then took us to the police station. There they emptied out the guilder bags onto a tray and the chief of police came in, took a sniff and said, "Hey. Good shit," and took two thirds of it to his office.

'The arresting officer rang a judge and interrupted the conversation to inform us that he was telling the judge we needed the weed to make our music. Both Jimmy and I went, "No we don't," and heard him say, "Yes, Your Honour, they do."

'Then we were led into the toilets and watched as they flushed what was left down the bog. Jimmy blurted, "But that wasn't all we had," and the cop gestured for him to shut up. The final irony was that Jimmy didn't have a carrot on him so I had to pay the fine, which came to about £1,000. They let us go immediately.

'As we were leaving, the cop handed something to Jimmy and said, "You sleep tonight." It was a bud he had obviously saved from the last guilder bag.'

These days, because we're habitual smokers, smoking no longer poleaxes us.

'Our tolerance is pretty high,' says Robin. 'I can't remember a time when I've been floored by it in recent years.'

Neither of us has gone for very long periods without weed. 'I had to give up when I contracted pleurisy,' says Ali. 'The first night of a pleurisy attack is the worst. We had been playing a live radio gig in Brighton or Portsmouth, one of those south coast towns, and my lung collapsed after we came off stage. The rest of the band were cajoling me into doing the encore, thinking that I was acting up as usual!

'After the gig I was carted off to hospital and was laid up for two weeks, but I only stopped smoking for two days. After that I'd have tiny drags on my spliff until I could get back into it wholeheartedly.'

Attitudes towards marijuana in the UK and rest of the west have obviously changed for the better, though there is still a huge conservative streak running through big business when it comes to weed. When we were preparing the artwork for our album *Homegrown* – which came out just a couple of years ago – we were told by the record company that we couldn't have a weed-green cover, because the cannabis connotation would put off the big retail chains like Woolworth's.

We got the same reaction when our management took our version of 'Legalise It' for Virgin to consider as a potential single. They basically said, 'You're having a laugh, aren't you?'

One thing we should clarify here is that we've never really been into smoking hash, or, as we call it, soap.

'I can't see the point,' says Robin. 'You smoke it and end up with a massively sore throat and a headache. It's a totally different experience from smoking draw. Time was I would never have a joint before midday, then it was never before teatime and later on never before a show. Now my rule is not to have one three hours before we go on stage. That way I feel totally straight, even though I might not be! And I always have a draw before we go back on for the encore. That hits me because I haven't had any for nearly five hours by then.'

We each have different views on smoking during recording

sessions. 'I'm not sure it enhances your creativity, although it makes you enjoy the music more,' says Robin. 'You listen to it differently. I smoke in the studio all the time, but during actual recording I cut back by half. When it comes to recording, making music stoned would be like doing it while you're drunk. Not a good idea. You become tune-blind.'

Ali feels that his vocal performance is more relaxed when he has a spliff. 'It's good for my performance if I have a toke before a take. On our new album *Who You Fighting For*, you can hear me spark up a spliff just before the track "The Sins of the Fathers" starts.'

We still smoke quite a lot: Ali around an ounce a week and Robin about a half an ounce.

'When I was in Jamaica me and my crew would get through a pound a week,' says Ali. 'When you're there you can smoke it neat because it's everywhere, buds lying on the floor of the house. Here it's £150 an ounce but over there it's so cheap.'

Last year Ali bought a vaporiser which ionises the weed. 'Effectively there is no smoke, which will help me cut my usage of the devil weed tobacco,' he says. 'Contact with pure nicotine would kill you within seconds whereas the only way weed is going to kill you is if a ton of it drops on your head!'

'I found it more depressing when my eighteen-year-old son took up tobacco, because I know what he's sentencing himself to,' says Robin. 'And alcohol is so much more harmful. I'd much rather my kids hang around with a bunch of dope-heads than lager louts. I've never been chased down the road by dope-smoking hippies!'

We don't think either of us has ever had a really bad time on weed. There have been times when we've been so stoned we couldn't talk, but that's usually quite a funny experience.

When Duncan was working in Barbados, Robin took a holiday to visit him. 'I was with my girlfriend waiting for him at his local bar, a little shanty hut owned by a geezer who opens his door

and sells liquor,' says Robin. 'This guy came over and greeted me
as Duncan's brother. He asked me if I wanted to go round the
back for 'a chat'; wary, I declined. Then he muttered something
about a smoke so we went and these other guys had a joint about
a foot long, wrapped in banana leaves. It looked just like a corn
on the cob and was ridiculous, the strongest thing I ever had.
The third time it came round to me I managed to say, "No
thanks," and then staggered back to the front. My girlfriend asked
me how it was and I just couldn't get a word out. To me she
sounded like she was talking gobbledygook and I sat there mute.
The only thing I could do was stare.

'My girlfriend got really annoyed because I wasn't talking to
her and turned her back on me. Then the geezer came along and
gestured to me that they were having another one! I was so stoned
I couldn't even say, "No!"'

The next time Duncan went to the bar, the locals said to him,
'He's a nice guy your brother but him can't hold his weed!'

Things are definitely easier for weed smokers since it was reclas-
sified and the chief constables across the country changed their
practices and the way they deal with it. However, the world still
hasn't quite come round to our way of thinking. There seems to
be a lot of game-playing between the various European countries, with Germany putting a block on the Dutch-proposed liber-
alisation because VAT can't be collected. Weed's not like tobacco,
which needs to be grown at high altitude. Cannabis will grow
anywhere, in the snow, on the beach, in the jungle, in your back
garden.

That's why in Britain these days it is a viable cottage industry.
In the west country there's some beautiful, strong stuff being
grown, Dorset Death and Devon Cream. 'Try it, you'll like it,'
says Ali. 'Those guys are serious farmers. Becoming a farmer is
actually an ambition of mine.'

Ali has even investigated launching a range of clothing which
mixed hemp with luxury materials like cashmere and alpaca.

'Woody Harrelson's done well with his hemp clothing range. He's based in Hawaii, so he has access to poona, the best smoke in the world,' explains Ali. 'Hemp-based oils and cosmetics are beginning to take off, but it's the application to harder-wearing materials which needs looking at. Cannabis is a viable alternative to reducing the world's forestry for paper, because it grows a few times a year.'

Maybe we'll always pay the price for sticking our heads above the parapet on this issue, but we believe you have to stand up for what you believe in. Not that we take any credit for helping to speed up the legalisation of marijuana. 'We've only said what millions say every day in this and other countries,' says Robin. 'We reflect the opinions of our peers, the ordinary people, and the fact that the tide is changing is to do with them, not us. People like Bob Dylan didn't change anything; he wrote songs about the fact that the times were a-changing. All we have done is add our voice to what is already being said.'

When record companies become uptight with us for banging on about this, we can see that their considerations are commercial first and foremost. They would far rather have another *Labour of Love* than an album which rocks the boat.

But that's where they are wrong. If the lyrics and the mood of a record reflect what ordinary people are thinking, then we believe it will sell, just like *Signing Off* did. That wasn't saying anything new about unemployment, but it presented information about it in a palatable fashion. And that's hopefully what we do for the marijuana issue: discuss it and not preach about it.

17

Big Love

We were absolutely cream-crackered when we finally came off the road in 1994. We'd been living in each other's pockets for sixteen years, by which time most bands have split up.

The previous six years had been the making of us as a band, but were also nearly the breaking of us. By the end of that period we had been trapped in the on-the-road bubble – with some of us living the mad party lifestyle and reaching such a stage of consumption and excess that we lost touch with reality.

'I really, really never wanted to go on the road with the guys ever again; that's how I felt at the time,' admits Robin. 'The last tour was so hard and Ali's drinking was so heavy that it wasn't pleasant being on stage with him, let alone in the same hotel or tour bus.'

We all took a few weeks off and then held a meeting at DEP. This was our big pay day, the one we'd all been working towards.

'As far as I understood the situation, having come off the road after the *Promises and Lies* tour, I would never have to work again,' recalls Robin.

Around this time there had been an article in music magazine Q about the richest bands in Britain, and among the Top Ten was us, the UBs. Apparently we had a pension fund with a total worth of £35m.

Paul Davies, who had handled the band's business and personal affairs for two decades by that stage, sat us all down around the boardroom table and told us that we had several millions pounds already in the bank, and with money still coming in from overseas sales and royalties, we were looking forward to having tens of millions more flowing in our direction. Pretty mindblowing, huh?

If we hadn't worked our bollocks off in the previous six years we wouldn't have believed him, but the fact is that we had released a run of multimillion-selling singles and albums, and performed sell-out tours all over the world. We'd also taken all those 'years out' to take advantage of tax breaks. 'We really felt we'd earned it,' says Robin.

The on-the-road period had closed out when Ali and Robin reached number one in the UK again, this time with Pato Banton on his version of the Equals' 60s hit 'Baby Come Back'. Although the band were all heartily sick of each other by this stage, there was never any rancour about our success.

'I think most of them hated the song because it's a terrible mix and isn't really our sort of music, but they knew that anything that keeps our profile in the charts would be good for UB40 as a whole,' says Ali.

Robin adds: 'It also revitalised Pato's career. He's still working on the back of that, doing well all over South America. He's still a massive star in Brazil. Personally I'm quite proud of it because I think it's a great version.'

Then the decision was taken to pay all eight band members and manager Dave Harper a lump sum of £1.2 million each. Even after that, there were still many millions either in the coffers or on their way in pipeline royalties – as they're called – from

songwriting and sales in 'overseas territories', as the music business refers to other countries around the world.

'I had already looked around and found myself a fifteenth-
century manor house in Warwickshire, right in the middle of
England, real Shakespeare country,' says Robin. 'At the time it
belonged to Jeff Lynne of ELO and the Travelling Wilburys, but
he had barely lived there since he acquired it in the 70s. So there
was a bit of bartering by fax, and within a couple of days it was
mine for several hundred thousand pounds. I decided I would do
it up over the next couple of years and then live in it. The house
became my obsession as I restored it to its former glory.'

Meanwhile, Robin continued to live with Sindy and their kids
at his house in Moseley even though the relationship had hit the
rocks as she continued her party lifestyle. 'I kept on asking her
to leave but she wouldn't,' he shrugs. To cope not only with this
but also with the impact of finally coming off the road, Robin
would head for the familiar surroundings of the Bournbrook
Snooker Club on the Bristol Road in Selly Oak, south
Birmingham, which he bought in the late 80s.

'I did what was required of me as a family man and a father,
but withdrew to the club four or five days a week,' he says. 'It
was my retreat; the people who go there are normal people, like
the guys I worked with at Leyland.'

Robin also entered a period of hefty weed intake, smoking
doobies – joints unadulterated by tobacco. 'I put on twenty-odd
pounds, which I didn't notice until one morning I was shaving
and Michelin Man was looking back at me from the bathroom
mirror,' he says. 'In the end I had to reintroduce tobacco to my
spliffs because it was all getting a bit much. I was probably getting
through three ounces of weed a week. Not that I was smoking
it all; a lot of it would go to my mates, but that's how much I
was purchasing. It was skunk as well, proper gear. That's a hell of
a lot, at £500 a week. Now I've cut right back, and try my damn-
dest to keep it down to half an ounce a week.'

While Robin divided his time between concentrating on the house and seeking refuge from his loveless marriage at the snooker hall, the rest of the band took their own much-needed sabbaticals and indulged in a variety of projects.

At the time Ali and Bernie's relationship was also suffering. 'I had always been adulterous, but she put up with it for years because it was out of sight, out of mind,' he admits. 'I was completely out of it by that stage, hanging out in shitty pubs and going on regular benders, pubbing it, clubbing it and partying for days on end.'

In 1996 the band got together for a bit of a jolly. The year before the Sandra Bullock/Keanu Reeves action thriller *Speed* had been a big box-office hit, so the Hollywood powers-that-be took the inevitable decision to make a sequel. 'I Can't Help Falling in Love with You' was still massive on US radio three years after it had gone to number one, and the movie makers decided to rope not only the song onto the soundtrack but also us into the movie, where we performed a new song, 'Tell Me Is It True' (later to appear on our next album *Guns in the Ghetto*).

Unlike the first film about a bus with a bomb on it, *Speed 2: Cruise Control* was based on a cruise liner with a bomb on it. We played the ship's resident band in a couple of scenes.

The studio flew us all out to LA and we all had a few days in Hollywood, all expenses paid. Sandra Bullock turned out to be lovely and we duly sang our song and went on our way.

When the film came out the scene where we perform 'Tell me Is It True' is the last you see of us in the plot. Somehow, an eight-piece reggae band from Birmingham mysteriously disappears from an out-of-control ship, without a trace. But ours wasn't to reason why – we trousered the fee and settled back to enjoying life.

Ali took his £1.2 million tour earnings and entered one of the most creatively fertile periods of his life, although he was to pay the price in terms of shattered personal relationships and a series of scary encounters with hoodlums, dealers and murderous rip-off artists.

The success of 'Baby Come Back' had helped boost the prospects for a solo album by Ali, something he'd been talking about for a while. Robin says, 'I told him, "Tell Virgin you want £1m and don't accept anything less."'

Ali instructed Mick Cater, the member of Dave Harper's management team who became responsible for day-to-day handling of Ali's solo album, to structure the deal so that he would not be required to promote it. 'I was doing a solo album, not launching a solo career,' he explains. 'Because I was in UB40 I maintained from day one that I would not go out on tour in my own right.'

Mick Cater approached the record company, whose initial offer amounted to an advance of £350,000. Ali declined it. 'A month later he came back and said, "They'll give you five" – meaning half a million quid. I said, "Bollocks."'

Virgin eventually paid the £1m, which they agreed would be non-recoupable – in that the advance would not be set against earnings from records – and also tax-free. Ali was also advanced £800,000 to set up a new Virgin-backed label, which he called Kuff, as in a backslap upside your head. The plan was for Kuff to release Ali's solo work and allow him to nurture rising Jamaican talent.

Having scored this huge coup, Ali set off to Jamaica to work on finishing recording the album *Big Love*, which was made up of six tracks he had put together himself in downtime from the road, while the remaining four were written on the island. Contributors to the project included local artists and the PEG production team set up by Earl from UB40, Gerry Parchment and Patrick Tenhyu.

'Initially I went over with Brian, his wife and Bernie, although I was usually on my own there,' says Ali. 'The kids would occasionally join me during the school holidays.'

Robin sees Ali's Jamaican sojourn as his brother's way of coping with coming off the road. 'Ali was able to sit in the sunshine and work on music away from the rest of us,' says Robin. 'I was totally chuffed for him. Not only because it gave him a chance to do his own thing, but also because I knew that, as usual, any success he had would reflect well on UB40. By the time it came out, we had taken a year off, so we actually benefited from his visibility as an artist when his single and album were released.

'Although he would make the occasional threat to walk, it was clear to me that having the freedom to express himself would actually make him more secure within the band. I was as excited for him as I was disappointed when I heard the album for the first time. It was full of great tunes but I wasn't overjoyed with the production.'

'It sounded fucking great to me!' says Ali, for whom the move to Jamaica represented the fulfilment of a lifetime dream. For a period he conducted a relationship with the singer Pamela Starks, who he had met on the road. She joined him on the island for periods of time. 'I was particularly off my face then,' admits Ali. 'I was smoking all the weed, snorting all the cocaine and drinking all the white rum in Jamaica. I seriously thought I could have two wives; one there and one here. Obviously that didn't go down very well at home, but I was very selfish. It didn't matter who advised me, or the sense that they talked. I didn't know what I was doing. I thought I was enjoying myself but I can see clearly now that I was miserable. It's only when I cleaned my act up years later that I realised how unhappy I was then.'

Ali's unhappiness was exacerbated when he embarked on a complicated and ultimately abortive series of property and business deals. First he launched a joint-venture studio at Firefly with a high-profile local personality called Richard Sinclair.

Sinclair's father had been a Jamaican MP in Prime Minister Michael Manley's Labour government of the 70s and 80s, and father and son had extensive interests in the region, including a Caribbean supermarket chain.

According to Sinclair, the studios had been owned in the 70s by Ali's hero Bob Marley. The reggae superstar had secreted them away from the gaze of the Jamaican tax authorities under the guise of the Robert Nesta Marley Home For the Aged, but the project was not completed by the time of his death in 1981.

Sinclair told Ali he purchased the studio from the bank which handled the sale of some of Marley's interests. 'There was a beautiful recording room overlooking the ocean,' says Ali. 'I loved it there and invested a lot, refurbishing the whole place. I also installed $1 million's worth of equipment.'

That wasn't without its difficulties. Even though Ali was ploughing a huge amount into the island and providing work and income for local residents, the Jamaican legislation at the time enforced 100 per cent duty on imported luxury goods such as recording equipment, thus adding another $1 million to the exercise. Eventually, with the aid of Jamaican MPs Marjorie Taylor and Omar Davies, Ali managed to argue his case successfully and, in fact, the law was changed as a result of his endeavours.

'I still think it's wicked,' Ali says of *Big Love*, and, initially at least, the public agreed. The first single, 'That Look In Your Eye', did really well, reaching number five in the charts in May 1995, although it wasn't in fact the track he wanted released. 'That came out as a result of the machinations of Cater, Harper and the record label,' says Ali. 'The first I knew that it was a single was when I got a call telling me it had been released.'

Ali's refusal to promote the album contributed towards the growing friction between management and the record company, and his fortunes started to falter: a version of the classic pop-reggae cut 'Let Your Yeah Be Yeah' topped out at number 25 four months later and a duet with nine-year-old daughter Kibibi on the Frank and Nancy Sinatra standard 'Somethin' Stupid' only reached number 30 in December of that year.

'We shit all over the Robbie Williams/Nicole Kidman version which came out a few years later,' he chortles. 'But the problems with the record company had really kicked in by then. I found out they hadn't been informed of my decision not to tour the album live. When the message was eventually conveyed to Virgin, they were at a loss, just didn't know what to do with the album. In my opinion record companies are useless cunts!'

Big Love shifted merely respectable numbers when compared with the millions sold by UB40 in recent years, though the tainting Ali felt at that experience was nothing compared with the trouble heading his way.

18

Guns in the Ghetto

When Ali took up residence in Jamaica he was soon joined by his long-time roadie and soul-mate Pops. 'I'd known Pops since we were both about nine years old, when we were all kids together in Balsall Heath,' says Ali. 'He was one of the gang we ran with. He and I grew very close when he came to work for the band.'

Pops and our other long-time roadie Wingy had even been in a band together, Solid Vibes, who were managed by the people who ran the UB40 fan club, so we were all very tight.

'When he joined our crew in the 80s Pops and I became best buddies, inseparable; we dived in every ocean in the world together and he'd been at my side on so many tours. After I moved to Jamaica I got a call from him, all broken-hearted. He had split from his missus and had lost the house he had in Christchurch, New Zealand, so I told him to get himself over. He started working for me, on a regular wage with a great car and a nice house with a pool. That was the problem really. I paid for every-thing and he had no incentive to do anything.'

As well as Richard Sinclair, Ali had business dealings with a colourful Brummie also based on the island, the now deceased

Solomon Wine. For a while everything was hunky-dory as Ali threw himself into a variety of projects for Kuff Records.

Our brother Duncan even recorded a reggae album of covers at Kuff; some Jamaican tunes, 'The Man in Black', a folk song of our father's, the old Cascades' hit 'Rhythm of the Rain', even a version of Val Doonican's 'Walk Tall'!

'Duncan had been over helping me keep an eye on things,' says Ali. 'He has such a great voice it seemed a crime not to take the opportunity to make an album. It was great and Mick Cater promised me on his life that he would get Duncan a recording contract. By the time it was completed there wasn't a sign of any deal, so we had to shelve it. The album cost £150,000 and none of it has ever seen the light of day.'

That was the level of advances being paid by Kuff, and when records weren't released, resources became strained. Other artists who received Kuff advances of between £90,000 and £150,000 included Brit-reggae singer Bitty Maclean, Jamaican group F.O.U.R. and a reconstituted version of the 2Tone band the Specials, which didn't feature either mainman Jerry Dammers or frontman Terry Hall.

'Again I found out too late,' says Ali. 'They were signed by Cater and Harper for £90,000 without consulting me.' The resultant album, *Today's Specials*, came out in 1996 and failed to make its mark, while Bitty McLean's album *Respect*, a collection of covers of Otis Redding songs, was never released, a source of bitter regret for Ali. 'Bitty put his heart and soul into *Respect* – it's the best album I have ever been involved in,' he says. 'We delivered *Respect* to Virgin, but they just didn't want to know. I would love to see it released, and believe that one day its worth will be recognised. I don't even have a copy any more because I lent my remaining CD to Chrissie Hynde and she loves it so much she won't give it back!'

A Kuff recording that did hit the shops was *The Dancehall Album*, UB40's collaboration with established artists of the local scene such as Mad Cobra, Beenie Man and Lady Saw, while Ali was also working on a whole host of recordings with the legendary rhythm team of Sly and Robbie.

'They are the greatest,' he says. 'It was incredible for me – who had been a fan of their stuff for years – to be playing with such fantastic musicians. I can't praise Sly Dunbar and Robbie Shakespeare enough. I love them.'

Being in Jamaica also afforded Ali the opportunity to connect not only with Sly and Robbie but with the reggae pioneers who informed his youth: Toots Hibbert, Ken Boothe, John Holt, Aston Barrett, Ernest Ranglin, Augustus Pablo and others who were later to appear on the UB40 album *Fathers of Reggae*. 'All those guys would come and see me. I had to pinch myself sometimes,' he says.

The *Fathers* album, which wasn't released until August 2002, is one of the peaks of our career. It felt incredible that these gods, who we had worshipped and paid tribute to, should cover our songs.

'They could have told us to piss off and it wouldn't have surprised me in the slightest,' says Robin. But, practically everybody we approached jumped at the idea. What was really nice was that, after we'd talked to a few people, we started getting phone calls from other singers asking, "Why aren't I going to be on the album?"'

Gregory Isaacs covered 'Bring Me Your Cup' while John Holt did 'The Pillow'. Bob Andy sang 'Love Is All Is Alright', Ken Boothe did 'The Earth Dies Screaming'. Toots Hibbert recorded 'C'est La Vie' without a lyric sheet and improvised fantastically through the parts of the song he had forgotten. 'That's probably one of the best vocals I've ever heard,' enthuses Ali.

In consultation with the rest of the band, Robin matched the artists to the songs, deciding that the Mighty Diamonds would do 'You Could Meet Somebody' and Jackie Robinson would cover 'Don't Do the Crime'. 'It was very satisfying when an artist would say, "Who picked this tune for me? It's perfect,"' says

Robin. 'I can't believe we had the gall to even think of doing it. The only sadness was that Dennis Brown passed away before we had an opportunity to work with him.'

Kuff is also the place where we recorded the next UB40 album, *Guns in the Ghetto*. 'In many ways Ali was picking up where he had left off with his solo album,' says Robin. 'Having worked on *Big Love*, he was eager to get back to a UB40 project but, apart from Brian, the rest of us were still slowly coming out of that period of downtime.'

It was to be a long haul before the album was realised. The problem, says Ali, was that outside of himself and Brian, the rest of the band just weren't interested. 'Brian and I already had four songs which the whole band had recorded earlier and within three months we added another six,' says Ali. 'By then we had the basic structure for a new album, but it took another year for it to come out.'

Ali believes that certain members of UB40 resented the fact that he and Brian had made headway without them. 'They all came over for a week, listened to the demos, decided they didn't like them and then flew back,' he laughs. 'After a few more weeks in England, some decided that we had something after all and flew back out again! It was crazy! Paul Davies told me we spent £1m flying everyone back and forth to try and find out what they thought of it.'

After a lot of work we finally got there. 'Personally I loved the songs and was grateful to Ali and Brian for having worked so hard while the rest of us were doing very little,' says Robin. 'As far as I was concerned we had flown back that time to England to sort out some domestic stuff before returning to properly start work on the album.'

Despite the problems surrounding its creation, *Guns in the Ghetto* remains Ali's favourite UB40 album. 'It sounds like a reggae record, made in Jamaica, proper,' he says.

For Robin, a surprise awaited him on his return from the *Guns in the Ghetto* sessions in September 1997. While he had been away, Sindy had moved herself and the kids into the Tudor manor house Robin had been refurbishing for sale.

'I never had any intention of moving the family into the house,' he says. 'Sindy knew full well I wasn't prepared to do that and I thought she made a smart move to get in there while I was away. When I got back I had no choice but to move in myself. It was either that or lose the entire property to her.'

So started an unhappy period: the couple lived together for several years until a settlement for her to leave could be reached.

Back in the Caribbean, Ali was facing rumblings about who really owned Kuff Studios. 'There was all sorts of talk going down that Richard Sinclair – or Pussy Sinclair as I like to call him – didn't actually own it in the first place,' says Ali. 'The whispers were that the Marley Estate, which is very powerful on the island, were none too pleased. One night I went up onto the roof of the studio to find Sinclair in deep discussion with Rita Marley. I didn't even know she was in the building. They went dead quiet when I turned up.'

During the same period Ali had hooked up with Astro and Earl to convert a large house called High Heaven into a hotel. High Heaven is across the bay from the fabled Goldeneye, the place once owned by James Bond creator Ian Fleming which is now part of the chain of luxury hotels run by music business mogul Chris Blackwell in an area called Oracabessa.

'The irony is that I was at my saddest and most confused when I was at my richest,' confesses Ali. 'I soon discovered that people weren't too happy for me. For a while I was known back home as "Fat Wallet" among some of the other members of the band. Meanwhile, there I was in Jamaica with people shitting on me left, right and centre. A lot of skullduggery started to occur.'

Ali brought in Earl's production team, PEG, again, this time to produce an album for the singer Yazz, who had scored her own hit in the late 80s with the song 'The Only Way Is Up'.

Then he discovered that Patrick and Gerry tried to cut him out of the sessions behind his back. 'When they came over to Kuff we put the music down with me providing guide vocals for the songs Yazz was going to sing,' says Ali. 'They returned to London where they were supposed to mix it down and finish it. One night I got a call from Yazz complaining that she had visited the studio and discovered them mixing a record for Gregory Isaacs on her time.

'This was happening a lot. I was trying to help a lot of people out who I later discovered were going behind my back,' says Ali. 'Unpleasantness and jealousy were rife; it was pretty lonely. Added to that I was stocious most of the time, seriously off my face.'

As the sessions for *Guns in the Ghetto* came to a close, the wrangling over who actually owned Kuff intensified, with both Sinclair and Solomon Wine displaying divided loyalties.

'At one time when I was off the island Pops called to say that Wine had sent his bent police friends to wave guns through the fence at Orocabessa. They actually took pot shots at the building and Pops.

'I had gone into business with the two, I thought, biggest pussies in Jamaica. I've got to say that I also met some of the best people I've ever encountered in my life there as well – the likes of Sly and Robbie, Toots Hibbert, John Holt and my man Ken Boothe – but Sinclair, Wine and, as it turned out, Pops were, in my opinion, a right trio of twats.'

One day, in a highly organised and covert operation, Ali organised for the $1million's worth of studio equipment to be taken out of Kuff under the guise of gear that belonged to the rest of UB40, to which none of the locals would lay claim.

It was transferred to the top room of his house in Orocabessa, where a recording facility was set up. 'One time I was sitting on the bog and I could hear Toots laying down a vocal over Sly and Robbie's rhythms! My house!'

Here Ali oversaw such projects as the critically lauded *Orocabessa*

One album, which showcased new artists such as Mr Vegas and Elephant Man, both of whom moved on to create higher profiles for themselves in the UK and US charts. It also featured the talents of such artists as Chrissy D, Scare Dem Crew and Monster Shack Crew.

'That is a masterpiece, though I say it myself,' Ali adds. 'I came up with idea of using jungle rhythms with dancehall bass drum patterns,' he says. 'It was a hybrid that really worked, because I would take out the jungle beats once the rest of the music had been put down, and what was left was contemporary, full of space, but still reggae. . . if a little jazzy.'

Brian worked with Ali on Kuff, (which had been re-named Orocabessa Records), introducing such UK hip-hop acts as Wolfetones to the roster. Ali wasn't as keen. 'Not only were we getting away from the idea of a reggae label pure and simple, but I thought they were crap, to be frank, embarrassing music which made me wince,' he says. 'I was pretty down with Coolio, having played with him in Europe when UB40 did the Pop Proms. Brian badgered the life out of me trying to get a tape of Wolfetones to Coolio. I turned him down flat, telling him that was his thing, not mine, and I'd have been embarassed to play it to Coolio. Though they did become better after a while!'

Ali also brought UK artists over to work in Jamaica, among them B15 Project, cousin Angus's group. 'We lost them when Brian fell out with Angus during a phone conversation concerning publishing rights,' sighs Ali. 'They signed to another label and not only did their track "Girls Like Us" go to number two in Britain, but it received an Ivor Novello nomination and appeared on tons of compilations.'

Ali says that the gulf between himself and Brian over the running of the label became unbridgeable after one particular conversation. 'I've never pretended to be a businessman but one day Brian said to me, "You look after the music and I'll look after the important stuff." I said to myself, "You've got that back to front mate."

But I didn't say anything to him. I just lost faith in him and, for a long time, the label.'

Later Brian closed Orocabessa Records' operations down without even consulting Ali. 'So I re-opened it without even consulting him!' snorts Ali.

Eventually Ali's recording facility was moved again, to the cottages opposite High Heaven. By this time O. R. was slowing to a standstill and Ali had returned to the UK to prepare for promotional duties, including UB40's first tour in three years, for *Guns in the Ghetto.*

'Pops was supposed to be looking after everything for me, but as far as I could see he was just looking after himself,' says Ali. 'He did the same as Pussy Sinclair: as soon as I left the island any money that he made he kept for himself.'

For a considerable spell, Ali kept up payments for maintenance of his interests in Jamaica, but 'not a ras' flowed in the other direction. For months, years afterwards, even to this day, tales of dirty dealings continue to filter back across the time zones. Assets were stripped without Ali's approval.

Then Solomon Wine was murdered while on a trip to England. 'There were even stories circulating that UB40 had him killed because we fell out over business,' says Robin, shaking his head. 'How ridiculous! But if you get involved with people like that, a lot of wild rumours soon start to fly around.'

Pops remained on the island. He and Ali haven't communicated for a considerable time.

'I feel betrayed by Pops but, more than that, I think he let himself down,' says Ali soberly. 'He had a great opportunity to create a happy new life for himself but we all know what happens to people when they are handed everything on a plate. They take it for granted and can end up resenting the person who handed it to them. We had a lot of fun together but then it all soured. All he had to do was handle the studio when I came back to the UK but he fucked up.

'I'm disappointed in Pops. He could have been a success, because we had worked with everyone on the island and the studio could have been a great business. But the money dried up and when I stopped sending him £200 pocket money a week after seven years I think he started to feel hard done by. I'd become his employer rather than his friend and he'd be phoning up asking where the money was, when, in fact, he wasn't doing jackshit to make anything of the business there.

'It's ironic because, for a time, Pops had the life I wanted. He was in my house with my pool and my cars and my records. Not so much living the life of Reilly as the life of Ali!'

Nowadays High Heaven stands an empty shell, never completed, while Ali has written off any interest in Kuff Studios and the $1million's worth of recording equipment is now at another site. 'I'm happy that at least it's being used,' shrugs Ali. 'When we first went to Jamaica twenty years ago we stayed in gorgeous cottages in Negril, smoking buds of sensimilla which made you think you'd died and gone to heaven. Now the crack pipe rules on the island, Aids is rife, the roads are all mashed up. It's very sad.'

Another sadness is the homophobic content of a lot of dance-hall. A lot of the prominent artists seem to be obsessed with it. A couple of years ago the big song on the island – which went to number one there – featured a lovely melody and a children's choir singing: 'If you go to chi-chi man's bar, bring we fire, mek we burn. If you get in a chi-chi man's car, bring we fire, mek we burn dem. . .' Basically they're advocating setting fire to gay people.

'I think it's because they've got a problem with it, if you know what I mean,' says Ali. 'When the subject has been brought up in my company, I always ask, "Why are you talking about it so much? It doesn't bother me either way, so what's your problem?

'That makes them absolutely crazy, but I really do believe that people who go on about hating gays to that extent are in denial themselves.'

And it's not as if the issue is restricted to the reggae charts. There is a terrible statistic about the number of gay homicides every year in Jamaica, and it's generally accepted that a quick and efficient way of obtaining emigration papers is to tell the authorities that you are gay. They know that it can be a life-threatening condition on the island.

When Ali returned to England after his Jamaican adventure, our brother Duncan travelled over and closed up Ali's house, removing furniture and whatever else was left of his personal effects. In the following weeks the house was gutted and even the air conditioning stripped and sold. The house was bought by its new owners for a pittance. Ali hasn't returned to the island since.

Jamaica really is Dodge City and can be very hard work. 'You have to really want to live there to be there,' Ali sighs. 'It's been destroyed by the combination of the American dollar and cocaine. Half of the money that's made there goes into what they call "other business".'

Ali harbours no regrets about his Jamaican sojourn. 'I was lucky to have such problems in the first place,' he explains. 'I had a lovely house on the island and worked with the greats. If I started whingeing, some poor bastard in Jamaica without anything would be quite right to tell me, "Get a life."

'I was walking on hallowed ground. Experiences like recording at Bob Marley's old studio were among the most beautiful things that have ever happened in my life. I was doing what I'd always wanted: to make music that sounded like the reggae I love. *The Dancehall Album, Respect, Guns in the Ghetto, Orocabessa One* – these were all beautiful to me. I worked on six, seven albums, including one of Sly and Robbie's. It was a very productive time in my life, but unfortunately whenever I left the island or took my eye off the ball, my "buddies" seemed to me to be double-crossing me.'

Meanwhile, back at home a financial disaster of huge proportions was lurking just around the corner.

19

Money Matters

With *Guns in the Ghetto* completed, delivered to Virgin and ready to go, in the autumn of 1997 we were due to venture back on the road with an American tour on which, we were assured, we would make money.

Then the first of a series of bombshells broke.

Some months earlier we had given Dave Harper an ultimatum that UB40 would only continue to be managed by him if his partner Mick Cater was not involved in any way in booking our live shows.

We won't go into the reasons here, but, on the day we were due to leave for the US *Guns in the Ghetto* dates, we discovered that Mick Cater had been very much involved; in fact he had overseen the tour schedule. The crew had already left for the States but we took the decision to pull the tour, which upset a lot of promoters and venues. For us there was no choice in the matter: we had also discovered that the US tour was going to cost us money rather than make a profit. Even so, the cancellation of the dates cost the band several hundred thousand pounds in extensive rehearsal time and compensation to the promoters and venue operators for lost ticket sales.

Then we called Dave Harper up to DEP for a meeting and gave him the news: 'See ya.'

He pretty much knew it was coming, so that was that.

One of the saddest aspects of the *Guns in the Ghetto* experience is that we never got to showcase the album live. 'It would have been the best tour we'd ever done,' says Ali. 'We had rehearsed and rehearsed until it sounded fantastic.'

It was frustrating – as we licked our wounds and paid off the American live operators – to watch the album effectively wither on the vine, as records do if they are not promoted live. *Guns in the Ghetto* eventually sold one million copies; that may sound a lot, but it was a tiny fraction of the ten million copies sold by its predecessor, *Promises and Lies*.

This was the bad time for us. The unsettling signs threatening our dreams of long-lasting financial security began to mount up. Despite the fact that Paul Davies had assured us just four years previously that we had millions of pounds tucked away, there didn't seem to be enough cash around to pay the studio electricity bills, let alone run the international-standard recording facility which DEP had become.

One spring morning in 1998 Jimmy was woken to find the bailiffs at the door: his medical insurance bills hadn't been covered. Not good for the drummer in a band which had sold fifty million-plus records.

At one stage the studio was dark and several staff who had been with us for years were laid off without our consultation. Although the studios had not been utilised to their full potential during the band's prolonged absence – and the overhead was running at hundreds of thousands of pounds a year – it was definitely time to take action, especially since we had embarked on recording a third volume in the *Labour of Love* series.

We had a showdown with Davies, who told us that the cash-flow shortage was due to the fact that the band's huge nest egg was locked into a number of high-interest pension funds. These had been negotiated by the best – and most expensive – blue-chip accountants in the world. We knew that much, because we'd paid these companies huge amounts to look after our money for us.

After twenty years in the business we deemed ourselves a band of spliff-smoking wandering minstrels who provided for the extended UB40 family, made up of partners, ex-wives, children, and in some cases grandchildren. As musicians and writers foremost, our main concern was to be world-class entertainers, not bank managers.

Even so, it was becoming crystal clear that something was wrong with the UB40 finances. We took the decision to have the co-author of this book, Timmy Abbot, on board to look after management, given his experience with the likes of Oasis, Robbie Williams and Fatboy Slim.

Meanwhile the books and business affairs were taken over by a couple of local financial experts who came highly recommended: Lanval Storrod and Dave Parker. They announced that they would carry out a thorough audit of our affairs.

At a band meeting a few weeks later Lanval and Dave broke the news: there was nothing left in the pot. Not the millions we had been told were ours to live off for the rest of our lives.

Nothing.

We were borassic.

Again.

Since it was clear that huge amounts of money had been mismanaged, one of the huge financial conglomerates paid us back their considerable accountancy fees without any argument, but to this day we do not believe Paul Davies, who was after all the individual responsible for our finances, acted improperly. We both believe that the dire straits were caused by his incompetence which spiralled out of control.

And, as if it couldn't get any worse, it soon became clear that, if we didn't move fast, our entire catalogue of songs, which we owned, would be auctioned to the highest bidder to pay off the mountain of debts.

We avoided that by persuading Virgin to step up and kick in sizeable backing in exchange for extending our contract with them.

We've always shared the same philosophy: even though it's twenty-five years later, all we are is a bunch of unemployed blokes lucky enough to be playing the music we love. So no matter what has gone wrong we've loved every second of it and had a great life. We've never even come close to splitting up. Neither of us can remember one occasion when somebody has said, 'That's it, I've had enough.' Even the Beatles can't say that – Ringo walked out for a week not long before they eventually went their separate ways. Through all the peaks and troughs not once had any member of UB40 said, 'I'm off.' Faced even with this catastrophe, we decided to carry on. . . regardless.

20

A Close Encounter of the Kray Kind

One night during his bingeing days, Ali was carousing in the Portland Club in Brum when this guy approached him with a guitar.

His name was Pete Gillette and he had a thousand-yard stare. Hardly surprising: he'd just come out of nick after seven years with Reggie Kray and was mad to play this song they had written together.

Called 'Closet Queen', it went:

> You act so macho and manly,
> All through the day,
> But in the hours of darkness,
> You're the other way!

Then came the chorus:

> You know just what I mean:
> You're a closet queen!

In Ali's drunken stupor his donkey ears popped out of his head and he declared to the guy, 'I'll produce that for you!'

The next day they reconvened at DEP and Ali laid down the track. 'It was really wicked actually, and made the song sound as funny as fuck, but after a very brief while I completely lost interest.'

Soon afterwards a letter arrived. It read:

Thank you Ali for looking after my pup. It's a great thing that you're doing and I really appreciate it.
God bless,
Your friend Reggie Kray.

What did Ali do? 'I *deffed* it, didn't I?' he says. 'What else are you going to do when you receive something like that?'

Not long afterwards the second letter arrived:

Dear Ali,
My friends say you have been taking the piss, and I've heard you are not helping the pup. Remember this: you kick the pup, you kick his master,
God bless,
Your friend Reggie Kray.

That was enough to get back into the studio. Suddenly Ali found a window in his busy schedule and finished the track. 'I thought I'd go the whole hog and get the sound of a whip in there during the chorus,' says Ali. 'But I couldn't find a good enough sound. This is how desperate I was to placate Reggie. I went through 'Rawhide', 'Xanadu', any song with a whip sound on it, but I ended up using a BBC sound effects recording of an arrow flying through the air followed by somebody being slapped around the arse! Put a bit a reverb on it, and how's your father. Then at the very end I put a gunshot on it, just to round it off nicely.'

The record was duly delivered and the third letter arrived:

Dear Ali,
Thank you for finishing the record.
A photograph of your band now hangs above my bed.
God bless,
Your friend Reggie Kray.

Ali breathed a long sigh of relief and retired his tartan donkey ears for ever.

21

On the Road Again

With the new team in place at DEP we could concentrate on doing what we do: playing music. Having completed *Labour of Love III* by the late summer of 1998 again we set off, traversing the world, playing everywhere from Australia to Yokohama to Venezuala, via Melbourne's Metro Club and KIIS FM's *Wild Wild Wango Tango* show in Los Angeles.

The first single from the album, 'Come Back Darling', sold enough to get into the UK charts at number seven, a major boost to our battered morale. Maybe, we thought, we can do it all over again.

Virgin seemed to put their weight behind the record and we carried out promotional activities we'd never have considered before. There was even an album playback at ritzy Leicester Square club Sound Republic which was incredibly well received by the crowd of record execs, radio pluggers and press who packed out the venue.

It is strange to think that, for a band that had been going for two decades, this was the first time we'd ever done an industry showcase, but we realised that such events were now an integral part of the business, and the glad-handing continued when we we went out on the road promoting the album.

One night in New Jersey we played a festival alongside Britney Spears, who was then well on her way to becoming the newest and biggest pop star. 'I thought to myself that my kids would never forgive me if I didn't get her autograph,' says Ali. 'As it turned out, word came down from her management that we were to be summoned to her dressing room because she was such a fan of the band. Apparently "Red Red Wine" is one of her favourite records.

'A black bouncer larger than nature itself escorted me to her dressing room. As for Britney, she was smaller than anything I've ever seen.'

The *Labour of Love III* tour took us from an encounter with the miscroscopic American pop superstar to one of the most unusual gigs of our careers. At the time we were due to perform at the Miss World ceremony in Mauritius and then move on to South Africa and Nigeria, but those gigs were bumped and, because there was a problem between agents and promoters over tour advances, it was decided that the safest thing to do with five and a half tons of our equipment floating around the Pacific was to head for India, where we were booked as part of the Filmfare Awards, the Bollywood movie industry's equivalent of the Oscars.

We flew into India from Dubai one day in February 1999 and visited the promoter's incredibly lavish house in the middle of Bombay. There was tabla recital and all the beautiful people were out in force, with amazing vegetarian food and Cartier cutlery, indoor fountains, all of that.

And yet, right bang outside the gates of the house was the most abject poverty: starving children, some of them missing limbs and blind. Sometimes it's very difficult to square that when you're in a band staying in the lap of luxury.

We felt very welcomed by the Indian people and concentrated on making the Mumbai show really special. Not only were there going to be fifty thousand people at the huge Andheri Sports Complex, but Rupert Murdoch's Star broadcasting network was beaming the show live across the world to an audience of more than half a billion people.

We all went to an upmarket part of Mumbai and bought ourselves the finest silk shirts and traditional Indian trousers for the performance, only to be told by the Indian fans that they wanted to see us in Western designer gear. 'Why you dress like bloody Indian?' they demanded.

There were black-capped Indian SAS guarding the front row since there weren't only all the stars of Bollywood in attendance but also some serious politicos as well.

When we found out that the audience would also include Asha Bhosle – the absolute superstar diva of Bollywood soundtracks who has made hundreds of albums and was the subject of the Cornershop hit 'Brimful of Asha' – we made contact with her management to see whether she would perform with us as well. The answer came back: she would be delighted.

'I rehearsed with her the day before,' recalls Ali, whose armed bodyguard, a Sikh, also provided us with some serious temple balls – the *bhung* used in certain religious services. 'We worked out this routine so that when we performed our new single "The Train Is Coming", Asha would come onstage and add some of the fantastic chanting that comes from the girls who work the tea stations. When she did it during rehearsals I nearly burst into tears, it was that beautiful.'

Asha told us she was very nervous about performing with UB40, but we assured her it would be OK. Come the night, and there was no sign of her as we went into our last song, 'The Train Is Coming'. Just as we hit the final chords, we got the signal that she had arrived and was ready to go. It turned out that it took Asha three hours to get through Mumbai to the show, because her car was stuck in a traffic jam behind an elephant.

But it was far too late.

We were ushered off stage and the show cut to some very camp Russian tumblers, who emerged from beneath the stage holding each other by their skulls and going through all sorts of weird calisthenics.

All we had time for was a quick 'goodbye' to Asha as we rushed away. We had three hours to catch our plane out of there and – wouldn't you know it? – we missed the flight because we were stuck in a traffic jam behind the same elephant that had held up Asha!

But at least we can say that UB40 have shared a stage with Asha Bhosle, even if it was for a few seconds as we passed each other.

While we were in Mumbai we shot the video for 'The Train Is Coming'. Two days of heavy scouting by the director Roger 'The Dodger' Pomphrey and his crew resulted in a video which is more like a *National Geographic* shoot mixed with traditional Indian culture-meets-Steven Spielberg.

It was a stunning promo which reflected the colour and experience of being in the subcontinent but sadly the song only reached number 36.

Back in London we continued the promotional grind, performed 'The Train Is Coming' on *TFI Friday* and that spring went out again, playing everything from the Guinness Garden Party in Belfast to MTV's Hard Rock Live in New York.

Since 2001 was also the twenty-first anniversary of our first release, we put together the DVD *UB40: The Collection* with footage and interviews from the anniversary concert we played at – where else? – Birmingham NEC. There was also an interactive history where one critic said: 'UB40 are to reggae what the Beatles and the Rolling Stones were to American R&B – except that they have actually stayed true to their cause.'

Which was nice.

Despite the occasional plaudit from a journalist, we, like many other acts of our vintage, began to suffer from the tightly controlled airplay policies of commercial radio stations as well as Radio One.

'Fifty million records we've sold and they still won't play our new singles on the radio,' says Ali. 'We're annoyed about that; we want to get our music out there. What more reason do you need to carry on?'

22

Ali's Recovery

The decades of ragga living began to seriously catch up with Ali by the late 90s.

'The combination of cocaine and whisky became my biggest problem,' says Ali. 'At my worst, I was racking the lines out and drinking two-litre bottles a day. And I was at my worst for a long time. When there wasn't any whisky around I would literally drink anything: crème de menthe, angostura bitters, the lot. And that was in the morning, just to get to the airport.

'Being on the road became a vicious circle of drinking to get up, drinking to go on stage and drinking to relax after the gig.'

The rest of us were no angels. Certain of us could also drink for days and others had their brushes with hefty drug intake, which is why UB40 has two buses when we go on the road: Ali would be on the ragga one, where it was mayhem 24/7, and Robin would be on the so-called 'librarians' bus', where we didn't mind a smoke and a drink but entertainment revolves more around reading and watching DVDs.

As the public face of UB40, Ali has to bear a far greater pressure than the rest of the band, and, if truth be told, he's never been that comfortable with fame. 'Ali is basically a shy guy,' says Robin. 'In his social circle he's the centre of attention because he's a funny, entertaining individual when he's with people he knows and can relax around. But he has never enjoyed entering a room where he doesn't know anybody. For him that is a trial. He'll break out in a sweat and panic badly.'

Once we were booked to present a Sony Radio Award together, and undertook a shopping trip for new suits for the ceremony in the centre of Birmingham. 'By the time we got to the third shop it was obvious we were being followed,' recalls Robin. 'Outside there was a crowd gathering, screaming whenever he looked over at them. I watched him visibly fall apart. Whereas others would revel in it and enjoy themselves, he just couldn't handle it.'

When we left the shop the crowd had swollen considerably. 'A taxi happened to be driving past, and Ali shouted at me, "Get me the same as you're having!"' says Robin. 'He dived into the cab, leaving me not only to cope with the fans but also to buy him a new suit!'

The irony is that because Ali has always been a bit more reclusive, he is the one of us people are most interested in. 'I'll sign autographs till the cows come home, if only to devalue them,' says Robin. 'Ali will always try and sneak through a crowd without signing them, which actually makes him more sought-after.'

People always say they don't believe Ali is shy, because he looks so relaxed and gregarious onstage. That's down to his huge reserves of charisma. Robin believes that Ali's addiction was based on his need to escape from the pressures of work and the unpleasant aspects of life. 'In case you couldn't tell by now, we have very different personalities,' Robin says. 'I've never wanted to get off my face and avoid whatever is going on in my life.'

Ali's take on Robin is that he was just as affected by the boozy atmosphere of their upbringing, but it had the reverse effect. 'He's the other side of the coin,' says Ali. 'Robin's whole life is about *not* drinking to excess, whereas mine was all about getting as much down me as possible. In a funny way he has just as much of a problem with it as I had.'

One of the contributory factors was that, as the lead singer and thus the focal point of the band, Ali was surrounded by people in management and at the record label who were only interested in appeasing him, to the detriment not only of the rest of us but also of his condition.

'He's my little brother and I love him, and he was destroying himself', says Robin.

'I was very, very unhappy and had been out of control for years,' admits Ali. 'That lifestyle has a way of catching up with you, because you can basically do what the fuck you like. And there's forty-two people on the road relying on you, and thousands out there in the auditorium who have paid their hard-earned dunny waiting for you to hit the stage and entertain them. So you go off the rails, and, to be honest, I think you're a bit weird if you don't.

'Personally, I can't get my head around people like Robin and Jimmy sitting in their hotel rooms night after night ordering room service and watching movies on cable. In one way, that's a sin; you're only given so many opportunities in this life, and you should take them.

'But it destroyed my marriage, mainly because it wasn't something I gave a fuck about at the time. I was married to the lifestyle, married to coke, married to shagging groupies, doing what the fuck I wanted.'

Everybody in the band knew the state Ali was in, and we had all tried in our own way to confront him, but to no avail. Mom was worried but she didn't know the extent of it.

'She'd make the occasional comment but only really understood how bad I was when I told her about it after I cleaned up,' says Ali. 'It wasn't as though I would rack them out in front of her, obviously.'

These days Ali takes on board the problems that his addiction caused, but he also believes that the band's failure to successfully

Astro and Ali by the Volga (cabbages out of shot), Russia 1986.

Gone fishin'. Back row: Ali, John 'Pops' Dowling, diver, Robin.
Front row: Astro and Henry Tenyue.

Ali's home near Goldeneye:
'Unpleasantness and jealousy were rife.
On the whole it was pretty lonely.'

Ali & Grandma in Oracabessa, Jamaica,
1996.

Resting up at a temple during our 1999 world tour.
From left: Brian, Jimmy, Earl, Mickey, Ali, Robin, Astro, Norman.

In a highly relaxed mood during the 1989 recording sessions for
Labour of Love II at Miraval Studios in the south of France.
Photograph by Andy Earl.

Chrissie and Ali: 'With your voice and my looks we could go far!'

Ali and Julie: 'She loves reggae music so we have a common bond.
But over and above all that I love her.'

Robin cues up: 'I'm fully aware I've become the old fart of
the club, roosting in my private room!'

Robin with Amy and Matt in the Lake
District, on the way home from a holiday
in Scotland.

Matt and Robin

'It doesn't get much better than this!' Performing with John Mayer and Eric Clapton at Roger Daltrey's Teenage Cancer Trust gig at the Albert Hall, April 2005.
Photograph by Richard Skidmore.

Ali and the Dhol Blasters, Live 8, Hyde Park, July 4, 2005.
Our message to the G8 leaders was: 'Sort this disgrace out; we've had enough!'

Shots from the 2003 gig we played at the Ahoy Stadium in Rotterdam, which was later released on DVD as 'Homegrown in Holland'. *Photographs by Rob Verhorst.*

The Brother Blend: Relaxing in Hawaii, 2004.

address the issue may have been related to the complex dynamics of all of our intertwining relationships.

'In a way it was easier for some of the guys to say: "Ali's Ali, he'll never change",' he says now. 'It was their way of dealing with me, and that made it easy to point the finger when things went wrong. However, unlike certain other members of the band, eventually I stopped of my own volition, while they were forced to cut out booze and drugs because of health scares. That has made them bitterly resentful that they can't have a line or whatever, and that's the difference; I'm not eaten up about no longer doing that stuff because, when it came to it, I actually wanted to give it up.'

It was in 1998 that Ali finally faced his demons. His marriage to Bernie fell apart when his infidelities became too close for comfort.

'Somebody close to the band had witnessed my philandering and told her all about it,' he says. 'She didn't speak to me for eight months, even though we lived under the same roof. At least we had the advantage of living in a nice big house. She lived in one part and the kids would come through and see me in the other.'

It's strange to reflect that Ali's life with Bernie was a mirror image of our parents' marriage. Eventually she could put up with no more of him being on the road, or the drink and infidelities, just as Mom finally had enough of Dad in the mid-70s.

At the end of that eight-month spell, Ali moved out to be with his current partner, Julie. 'I even did exactly the same thing that the old man did when he moved out of the family home once in the 70s,' says Ali. 'He lived with this woman about a quarter of a mile up Speedwell Road, which made it very difficult for our mom. Then when I finally left Bernie, I moved Julie into a cottage with me about a mile away from my house because I wanted access to my kids. It was such a mistake. I was being selfish and thinking about seeing my kids, more than thinking about what Julie and Bernie had to go through living so close to each other.'

After a few months he and Julie set up home in a flat in London and Ali set about wrestling with his addictive nature. 'I'd reached a stage where I'd have serious blackouts if I had a drink, and totally forget what had happened. Julie wasn't going to have a pissed-up junkie living with her, it was as plain as that,' says Ali. 'She had to tell me many, many times but we got there. In my heart of hearts I wanted to stop.'

'When somebody is drinking that seriously, the only way for them to stop is if there is a will inside the person themselves,' says Robin. 'When Ali parted from his wife and was with Julie he started to get a grip. I'm sure Bernie tried to do the same thing and got nowhere because of all the baggage they carried between them. But this was a fresh relationship, which gave Julie the strength to do it. She challenged him and Ali, bless him, sought help.'

Julie and Ali had known each other for quite a while before they eventually got together. 'I'd known Julie since she was eighteen and I was twenty-four,' he says. She is now a fashion stylist, but she has worked in the music business, at one time for Erskine Thompson.

'Julie has always loved reggae music, so we have that common bond to start with,' says Ali. 'But over and above all that, I love her. She cured me of my promiscuity. I'd never, ever been faithful to anyone in my life before. Julie is my main squeeze and I don't squeeze anybody else!'

With Julie's help, Ali consulted Harley Street doctor Barry Grimaldi, on the recommendation of Timmy Abbot. Grimaldi has experience in treating addiction, particularly among musicians and managers. 'As soon as he received my blood-test results he told me that I had to dry out. I also underwent treatment by hypnosis and gradually whittled away at my addiction, cutting out the cocaine, whisky and all other spirits, cider and lager.'

Robin points out that Ali's recovery was placed under extra pressure by touring. 'Usually addicts are taken out of their social circle and removed from their regular haunts to help them break the addiction,' says Robin. 'Ali's problem was that he had to go back on the road, *with* his social circle. That must have been really tough.'

It took Ali two years to finally stop snorting coke. One of the most difficult aspects was when band members would offer him a line, even though they'd been told he was giving it all up.

'I stopped drinking spirits after making an arse of myself in Spain with Julie, arguing and talking shit,' he says. 'At the time Julie would bring me a tumbler of whisky with my tea in the morning. I think back and realise why I'd be sick every morning, halfway through brushing my teeth.

'After that incident in Spain I said to myself: "No more whisky." Then it took me ages to stop drinking beer. I went through a six-month period of not drinking at all, which was pretty lonely, being at the back of the bus with everybody merry around me. I'd be going: "Fuck me, is that what I was like?" That was pretty sobering.'

These days Ali allows himself one drink before he goes on stage. 'When I wasn't having that I found I couldn't actually smile,' he says. 'I'd get so nervous my lips would stick to my teeth!

'The first show I ever played totally clean was the showcase for *Labour of Love III* at Sound Republic in Leicester Square in 1998. It went OK but I didn't enjoy it because my nerves got to me. And that affected my overall performance.'

Ali doesn't intend to give up the red wine or spliffs just yet. 'What has been important is ridding myself of the really evil stuff which took over my life,' he says. 'Sometimes I still go over the top with wine but I know now that one glass for me is like three glasses for anyone else. That means that if I have a couple, it's the equivalent to other people drinking a bottle. I try to avoid drinking more than a bottle, but occasionally it will happen and I won't remember a thing in the morning. I do worry about going to social occasions and try and avoid getting into that situation where I become the nutcase that I'm not.'

When it comes to gigs, Ali used to drink a bottle of wine
before he went on stage but now it's just a glass of Rioja. 'I have
a routine whereby I only arrive just before the gig, enough time
to get acclimatised before going on stage,' Ali says. 'No more
hanging about and getting out of it.'

Regardless of his experiences, Ali still sees drugs as a matter of
personal choice. 'I think in their right place acid and magic mushrooms can be wonderful,' he says. 'I've had proper MDMA and
it was beautiful. But I believe you should do these things once
and only once, because that first time opens so many doors and
you're never the same again. If you carry on, all you're doing is
chasing that first glorious feeling. You're never going to get there
and you may well die trying.'

Ali's divorce from Bernie was finalised in 2003, and the close-
ness of the intertwining relationships within the band and all our
various partners meant that there was some fallout, not least since
Mickey is Bernie's brother. 'It was a bit messy for a time but we're
coming out of that now,' says Robin.

These days Ali is firing on all cylinders; at the time of writing
he has a new solo album pretty much in the bag, containing a
series of duets with a range of collaborators, including a version
of Stevie Wonder's 'Big Brother'. The omnipresent Sly and Robbie
will provide the musical backbone.

'I'm pretty much of a computer illiterate and have never been
keen on the whole technological side of recording, so working
live with a band which contains those two is like heaven to me,'
says Ali. 'Man, you want to hear them play in the studio.'

Among other tracks is a version of the Everly Brother's 'Devoted
to You', performed with Robin. 'That is wicked,' says Ali. 'The
brother blend is certainly to the fore on that one. It's going to
be a really varied project. I've done Gregory Isaacs's 'My Number
One' with Cheb Mami, the Algerian singer who has worked with
Sting, and Brian and I have written several originals.'

As well as the solo album Ali has plans underway for re-energising

Orocabessa Music Group: 'It will be a reggae label pure and simple,' he says. 'That was what Kuff was intended to be in the first place and now that reggae has such a high profile the time is right, maybe. . .'

With a house – which was regularly graced by the presence of Edward VII a century ago – in Dorset, Ali is happier than ever these days. 'I love it there,' he smiles. 'I always liked visiting places like Christchurch at weekends, but living down there has made all the difference. It's beautiful and loaded with history. Apparently Lillie Langtry was regularly fucked in the cottage in our grounds!'

Ali is looking forward to staying in the same place for a while. 'I've moved seven times in five years,' he says. 'Now I have a beautiful place where Julie has always wanted to live, and we're very happy together.'

'These days I've got my brother back,' says Robin. 'He's full of enthusiasm and energy. He's doing his best work for years, and some of the tunes he has written for our latest album are among the most beautiful of his career. For 98 per cent of the time Ali's a very nice guy, and that's fine, because for 2 per cent of the time we're all arseholes aren't we?'

23

Robin's Nest

Robin spends as much time at he can at his Tudor manor house in Warwickshire. 'I don't even take holidays,' he grins. 'I don't need them. Every day I walk around feeding my ducks and fish and could quite happily toddle around doing that for ever.

'I love the house and am absolutely besotted by it, but as it became an obsession it also became an obligation because the upkeep is never-ending. I was watching a thing on the English Civil War on TV the other day and worked out that my house was already fifty years old when that kicked off. It's a very fragile structure and has to be treated as such.'

There is always refurbishment to be done. 'I spent my first two years here walking around with a hard hat on,' says Robin. 'At first I was pinching myself, because I couldn't believe it was mine. As the years have passed I've been saying to myself: "I can't believe I'm spending this much money!"'

The setting is beautiful, with pheasants, foxes, all sorts of wildlife. The large lake in front of the house is a constant source of fascination. When he moved in, there were quite a few wild ducks there, and Robin has introduced various domestic and exotic varieties. 'Now I get all sorts coming to visit. A pair of Mandarins once landed on the lake and stayed for a while, which set me off buying some for myself. In Japan you see them everywhere, but not here.

'I also put a thousand koi carp in the lake,' he grimaces. 'What a mistake. I didn't know at the time but there's a heron sanctuary a couple of miles away, so within a few months they were over poaching all my fish, here using my lake as a takeaway! The carp were absolutely decimated.

'But – fuck me – I sound like Bill Oddie. That's enough of that!'

The surveyor who first advised on making the house good estimated that around £70,000 should be spent. Robin reckons he has now invested £1.25 million in the property, but recognises that concentrating on the house enabled him to detune after such an intense and protracted period on the road, though the plan to do it up within a few years was derailed by Sindy's decision to move in back in 1997.

'Since I had to stay – because I wasn't about to let her live there alone – we continued to live under the same roof right up until 2002,' he says. 'I was miserable as hell and seemed to spend the whole of the 90s asking her to leave.'

Robin has written quite a few songs about the turmoil of his relationship with Sindy, most notably 'Where Did I Go Wrong' from the *UB40* album and 'Bring Me Your Cup' from *Promises and Lies*.

'That was about Sindy's drinking,' says Robin. 'The most recent one I wrote about her was 'I Knew You', which appeared on *Homegrown*:

> I knew you before you knew
> Who you wanted to be.
> Now I see the new you
> She's a perfect stranger to me. . .

Robin and Sindy finally parted in 2002 and he reflects again on the similarity of his situation to that of his mother more than twenty-five years before. 'Just as Ali behaved like our old man and wouldn't leave his partner despite his philandering and drinking, so I was like my mom, waiting patiently for years on end for my partner to leave.'

These days Robin is with Luci. At one time she was UB40's backstage co-ordinator, handling wardrobe and the dressing rooms. 'She once described herself in a documentary as "UB40's Mom" because she looked after all of us,' he says. 'I knew and worked with Luce for quite a while before we became a couple, which is why we have such a good relationship,' says Robin. 'Ironically we met at a time in my life when I was looking forward to being on my own. Not that I was going to live like a bachelor, because I've done all that, all the clubbing, but I'd been negotiating the parting from my missus for so long I just wanted to be by myself.

'Then one night about a year before we finally got together, Luci was a bit drunk after a gig and made all sorts of advances which I politely declined. I took her to her room and bade her goodnight. The next morning, and for months afterwards, she was mortified with embarrassment. Gradually we started to talk and then it happened. It was such a surprise for me to find a woman that I really liked and wanted to be with just when I wasn't looking.'

Robin and Luci kept their relationship quiet from the band for a while so that her position wasn't compromised, and it only came out in the open when she gave up her job with the band.

'The fact that we are together will be such a revelation to the UB Loonies, the fan club,' says Robin. 'They all know of her, and have met her on backstage visits, but don't know anything about this! Luci's worried that they'll all hate her because now she's living with me, so it will be amazing news for some people.'

Luci has become the licensee and manager of Robin's snooker club, another of Robin's abiding passions. 'Snooker is like golf, more cerebral than physical,' says Robin. 'I admit it, I am obsessed. I was never good enough to be a pro, but I enjoy the world, which is a bit seedy, what with all the betting and the characters it attracts.

'When I got into it as a teenager it was exotic and forbidden, kind of the same thing as going to a blues. You met and mixed with the underbelly of society, but over and above that I just loved the game from the off. From my late teens I started playing people who were better than me for money, which was like paying for lessons. Suddenly I discovered it was nothing to do with potting balls, but about your approach and strategy. My philosophy is that two breaks of 30 or 40 will win any game. However, I do regularly have 40–50 breaks and I've scored 88 twice.

'When we came off the road after the *Promises and Lies* tour in 1994 I was at the club five days a week, living there and playing my socks off. For years I used a really old cue I'd bought off a very good player called Alan Atkins. One night at the club, after he had played a particularly shite game, he was so upset with himself that he was about to smash it to smithereens.

'I told him not to and he was that irate he said, "Give us a fucking quid and you can have it!" Of course I fished out a pound immediately. For years afterwards he kept on asking for it back but we'd made the deal, fair and square. But that cue was an absolute nail, full of lead, as heavy as Christendom. So when I was playing all the hours God sent down at the club I developed this peculiar action which eventually dislocated my wrist. One of the bones would regularly pop out, and I'd be sat there massaging it back into place. Then I started wearing a brace; it was driving me mad so I decided that I had to replace that bloody thing.

'These days I've got a very special cue, stunning it is, hand-made by this guy who has a cottage industry in them, Mac Chambers.

'I was looking through his selection and couldn't find one that

I liked. Then I came across this beautiful cue with red African wood spliced into it. It was maple, not ash, which has a grain and can splinter, catching on your chin as you shoot. This absolutely smooth maple cue was perfect for me, because it also had a thin butt, and I have relatively small hands.

'I asked him about it and Mac told me it belonged to him, so he made me one exactly like his, with the same balance and weight. It cost me around £300 and I had a blue snakeskin case made by Cheddar Classics.

'The level at which it is played among the top people is all about clearing the table. They make 100 breaks in their sleep, whereas I've never made a 100 break in my life. But I have won a lot of money.'

Robin has also sponsored professionals. 'One of my best pals goes by the pro name of Jelly Baby,' says Robin. 'His real name's David Holt and he's a pool player, a right little hustler. But he did once win the UK Championship. I have won money on him but I have also lost, the biggest bet being around a couple of grand. Still, I've won the same amount a few times.'

There are nine tables and a bar at Bournbrook, which also contains a very private room for Robin and his mates. 'Otherwise I'd never be able to finish a game!' he exclaims. 'Business has been up and down over the years, in keeping with the popularity of snooker. When I first opened, it was packed out, and we have had great times with all the pros, people like Jimmy White. Jelly's very tight with him, Ronnie Wood, that circle.

'I know Jimmy pretty well and think the world of him. We've had a lot of fun together at the club and at tournaments around the country. A lot of the pros and people from that world just drop in if they're in town, people like John Virgo, Cliff Thorburn, Steve James. Every time Robby Foldvari, who is the world billiards champion, is in the country he practises in my private room. Of the rest of the band, Astro's pretty keen on snooker. He's got his own table at home and he often comes down to see me in the private room, while Ali – considering he's only really got one good eye – is pretty good at potting. Put him on a pool table and he's in his element.

'That room has one the best club tables in the country. For a start it's made of oak instead of mahogany, and it's Victorian, steel-backed and underheated to stop dampness slowing the game down. That table plays like a dream.

'I'm fully aware that I've become the old fart of the club, roosting in my private room with everybody coming to me to chat and play. I'm like the old geezer I learnt how to lose money from when I was a cheeky eighteen-year-old. He seemed ancient to me then, when in fact he was in his fifties! That guy was still teaching me stuff in his seventies. It's only a few years ago he stopped coming to the club. That's the beauty of the game – you never stop learning.

'It's only dawned on me in the last year or so that that is what I have become, playing all these young lads who could play me off the table in terms of skill but haven't got the experience at table-play. They don't understand why they can never get a shot when they come into my territory.

'I do think that the best player around these days is Ronnie O'Sullivan. He's the most gifted and natural we've ever seen in the game. He seems to know instinctively what others take years to learn, and what some will never understand. As long as Ronnie keeps playing I'm sure he'll break every record out there.

'I'm not one for going out drinking and carrying on like a proper pop star, but prefer to relax with a small circle of friends. I can go down to my local and have dinner and nobody will bother me. Still, the old cliché about fame being good for getting a good table in a restaurant holds true.'

Robin also has his own way of dealing with public recognition. 'As I've already said, I have developed this shell which gives the impression that I'm not really approachable. If you look like you don't want to be disturbed, most people won't bother you.

Not that I don't like the attention. If you walk around with a big smile on your face and exude a welcoming, open attitude then you're going to attract attention all the time.'

Generally, for pop stars, recognition goes in peaks and troughs, just like our career. When 'Swing Low Sweet Chariot' was chosen as the anthem for the 2003 Rugby World Cup that meant our visibility was raised, and so the recognition factor went up. Probably the only aspect we enjoy of the troughs is that nobody bothers us while we're in them. Our personalities aren't addicted to attention.

Ali believes that an aspect of Robin's character which isn't usually acknowledged is his insecurity. 'Despite his air of assurance, I know that he's as riddled with worries as the rest of us,' adds Ali. 'Not so long ago I watched him as he went to sing his number 'Sweet Sensation', at the NEC. He couldn't get through it quick enough. Robin will be the one soundchecking his instrument all day and then all through the gig, every night, even though he has his roadie, Animal, to look after that side of things.'

Robin was fifty on Christmas Day 2004, but in typical style didn't want a fuss made. 'I didn't see it as a landmark, just another birthday, so made it known that I wasn't up for any big surprises and had a lovely time with Luci and my two kids. That suited me fine.'

24

Family Today

Having divorced many years ago, Dad lives in Kilkenny in Ireland now while Mom is in Moseley. Dad released twenty-odd albums and was one of the most lionised people of the folk movement, but he's given up the road, though he sings down the local for free. They've got that folk music tradition over there, which suits him down to the ground. People like the Dubliners still turn up at our gigs just because they respect him so much, talking about 'yer da'.

Dad has suffered from various ailments, including cancer, which has now cleared up, thankfully. However, given the geographical distance between us all, we don't really see that much of him.

We are in contact when he comes back over to England for his medical tests, but because of his lifestyle and the fact that he's in his seventies, his health isn't tip-top.

Dad has stopped smoking now, though his lungs are knackered. In fact, when he was told he had cancer the doc said: 'I wouldn't worry about that because the emphysema will kill you first!'

At our granny's ninetieth birthday party a couple of years ago,

Dad was unhappy because we didn't get up and sing, the same old gripe going back to our childhood. We don't go to many of those gatherings but we were both certainly going to make it for our gran. Even so, the old man told Ali's girlfriend Julie: 'I bet you had to make him come along to this, didn't you?'

For Ali, the similarities between his and Dad's personalities have really hit home in recent years: 'It is uncanny to me how we have behaved in the same way not only in our married lives but with the drink and the road.'

The closest either of us has been to visiting Dad in Kilkenny was one time a couple of years ago when Robin was in Cork and tried to get a message to him, only to find he was over in Birmingham!

Mind you, it's good to know that he is in Ireland because we love the place. One of its charms is that it's so small and everyone talks so much that everybody knows your business. One year the band spent six weeks rehearsing for an album, hiding away in a little bed and breakfast in a village called Cappa Quinn west of Waterford in Kerry, where the true events behind the book and film *The Magdalene Sisters* actually took place.

We tried our very best to keep a low profile but every Friday night every pub in the area was packed to the gills because they all wanted to say hello to the UB40 boys.

Mom complains that Moseley doesn't have the village-like atmosphere of the past, bohemian and groovy, the place Tolkien used as material for *Lord of the Rings*. Our brother Dave lives with his partner Lisa Anderson, a high-flier in the UK music business who was the first-ever female head of a British record company and even briefly managed Geri Halliwell. They and their kids live in a beautiful timber-framed house with a duck pond in Kent. As well as running a folk club in London and handling various projects such as being product manager for a solo album by one of Dire Straits, Dave has been the house husband throughout Lisa's career.

One of Lisa's achievements was making the Brit Awards the glorious affair they are today. She was appointed in the wake of the fiasco in 1988 – when Mick Fleetwood and Sam Fox proved to be such mismatched presenters – and turned the whole thing around. Lisa wanted UB40 to appear to receive a lifetime achievement award in her first year but we felt that it was too soon in our career. That's a regret because we could have helped her out.

Robin still sees a lot of our brother Duncan, who is also a snooker addict, and a regular at Robin's club. 'Duncan's not as good as me, but he's close,' points out Robin.

Duncan has done all sorts: he's been an extra in *The Bill* and *Eastenders*, a chippie and a croupier. At one time Dunc got involved in opening a bar in Spain. It saw the worst rain in thirty years and the place was nearly washed away. They spent two weeks cleaning it up and the night before the grand opening it was revealed that he and his mate actually only owned a 49 per cent share and that put the mockers on that.

Last Christmas he went off to Thailand with our snooker-playing mate Jelly Baby to look into opening a beach bar there. They stayed with a friend on a little island . . . off Phuket. On Boxing Day morning they were sat overlooking the bay when a house floated past! The next thing Dunc knew the water was rising fast around the table they were sat at and all of them scarpered to the other side of the island, which had been absolutely devastated. Fortunately for Dunc and Jelly, the house they were staying in was one of the few still standing after the tsunami hit. Virtually everybody else they came into contact with had lost somebody.

Duncan arrived home four days later, not only traumatised by the experience but pretty disgusted by the behaviour of the English tourists, who were still demanding their drinks and meals amid all the carnage.

We don't know what Dunc's next adventure will be, but it's bound to be action-packed. You should read his book when it's done!

25

Silver Jubilee

One of the reasons UB40 is still around is that we have experienced failure, massive doses of it. We have never been consistent commercially, and, as you'll know by now, in between the highs there have been the flops. Maybe that's our problem: we've never gone into the studio and tried to replicate the successful formula.

Although we only seem to score a number-one hit every decade or so, (to date, fifty top 40 singles), our singles still sell well, which is why we're right up there with people like the Beatles, the Stones, Status Quo and the Bee Gees in terms of number of weeks our records have spent in the charts.

That has become quite a heritage to live up to, but our manager, Bill Curbishley – who we appointed last year – has plenty of plans for the band. He's a real heavyweight who has worked with the Who for years and handles people like Judas Priest and Jimmy Page, Robert Plant and the Led Zeppelin catalogue. Bill was also involved in *Tommy* and *Quadrophenia*, two of the biggest pop films ever.

As this book goes to print we have just kicked off our jubilee celebrations with a gig at the Albert Hall as part of Roger Daltrey's annual series of concerts to raise money for the Teenage Cancer Trust. Eric Clapton joined us on stage with his pal, blues guitarist John Mayer, for our set which consisted of 'I Shot the Sherriff', 'Food for Thought' and 'Kiss and Say Goodbye', the single from our latest album.

'He was a total pro and a complete gent. We had a blast,' says Robin. 'Eric played brilliantly after just one rehearsal.'

Roger Daltrey was also a total pro. He came up to DEP for a day of rehearsals, and then we ran through again with him at the Albert Hall on the day of the gig. Come the night, though, Roger felt that he just couldn't do it justice and pulled out of the performance.

The show itself was very well received and the *Evening Standard* gave us one of our most glowing reviews of recent years.

Reggae has been enjoying another revival over recent years, thanks to people like Beenie Man, Shaggy and Sean Paul having massive crossover hits in the States as well as here, and we know that by releasing projects like *The Fathers of Reggae* we've done our bit in keeping interest in it alive.

So we'd love to pay the ultimate tribute to the island which inspired us by playing live there, but there have always been logistical problems. 'It's coals to Newcastle isn't it?' points out Robin. 'If you can't do it properly there's no point going, and there has always been pandemonium at Jamaican events like Sunsplash, with people storming the venue because of ticket prices and shots being fired.'

Ali has a particularly bad impression of the Jamaican live scene. 'One day I visited reggae artists Derrick Harriot and Tommy Cohen backstage during a huge festival in Kingston,' he says. 'All these kids had basically crashed through the barriers and there were pitched battles taking place between audience members and the armed security guards. As we were chatting, this kid broke into the backstage area. A security geezer walked across to him and, in front of us, raised his gun to the kid's head and capped him, right there and then.

'We were all absolutely stunned. This kid died at our feet. It was the most shocking thing I have ever experienced in my life. What do you do? We all just edged away in terror but for that guy it seemed to be a run-of-the-mill occurrence. One of the other security guys came over and turned the body over with his foot: "'Im dead, yu know?" he said casually.'

That is one of the reasons why we would only ever play a free concert in Jamaica, or at least one where the money goes to Aids awareness, Unicef or a local good cause. Having tickets which are priced out of the pockets of most of the people in Third World countries always leads to bother. The value on human life is pretty low, and the people guarding those gigs would just as soon kill somebody as let them see the concert for free.

Bill renegotiated our deal with Virgin Records and we went back into the studio last autumn to record our latest album, *Who You Fighting For?* From the get-go it was decided that we needed to return to an organic rather than overly technological or computer-generated sound, because we truly believe people respond better to instruments being played live.

The two previous albums – *Cover Up*, which came out in 2001, and *Homegrown*, which was released two years later – were dominated by Jimmy and Earl's insistence on using computer-generated rhythms as the basis for tracks. 'It sounded uninspired,' says Ali mournfully. 'We had finally stopped recording as a band and that had an impact on the sound. What upsets me is how egos got in the way; the musical differences were really ego differences. Every bloody band splits because of "musical differences" when it's not about that, but money or personal stuff.'

One of the things we discovered about the songs on those heavily programmed albums was that, by the time we had repeatedly played them live, they sounded fifty times better than on record. That's because we had settled into the songs, shifted things around and let them breathe.

The title track of *Cover Up* was recorded in support of the United Nations campaign against Aids, and in 2001 we took the message back to South Africa, where the government's practice of 'denialism' – President Mbeki's refusal to accept that HIV, leads to Aids – has led to rampant infection and the loss of five million lives over the years. We played a number of dates there with Afro-pop star Ringo Madlingozi, who also recorded his own version of the single with us.

'Cover Up' was not only about wearing a condom to protect yourself from infection, but also about the fact that the Aids problem is all too often swept under the carpet.

This is a global epidemic of massive proportions and we felt that we had to let people know that essentially it comes down to economics. The people have been lied to, which is the biggest cover-up of all.

We dedicated our opening concert in Cape Town to the deceased South African child Aids activist Nkosi Johnson and also featured in a TV ad encouraging safe sex.

The follow-up single to 'Cover Up' was 'Since I Met You Lady', which featured dancehall diva Lady Saw. She was shunned by Radio One until she had a hit a few months later with No Doubt. One of the programmers there told our pluggers that they didn't play 'that sort of thing'.

Says Ali: 'It makes you wonder sometimes why you should bother consciously trying to make music that will be palatable to radio people. We realised long ago it was better to do our own thing and if enough people like it, then we must be doing something right.'

The follow-up to the *Cover Up* album was 2003's *Homegrown*, where, on the track 'Just Be Good', we took a pop at US president George Bush while the song 'Young Guns' took the gangsta-rap

likes of 50 Cent to task for glorifying gun crime. We know for
sure that young guns never grow old.

With hindsight we now realise that *Cover Up* and *Homegrown*
suffered from our approach not just to production but actually
recording. Our music is organic and has to be treated as such.

'I'm obsessed about UB40's music, always have been, always
will be,' says Ali. 'Some might think that maybe I'm too precious
about it but I can't be any other way.'

When we started to rehearse and record in the winter of
2004–5 it was clear we were working as a unit again. For the first
time in years everything seemed to gel and everyone was enjoying
themselves again, with Jimmy and Earl agreeing to give up their
obsession with electronic beats and samples and actually playing
their instruments. After the lost electro years it sounded great.

'For a long time I think we disappointed ourselves,' admits
Robin. 'Some of the records we made in the late Nineties and
early Noughties weren't as good as they could have been, which
is probably why they didn't sell as well. People started to talk
about us as if we had retired, but last year we played Europe,
Australia, New Zealand and Hawaii and sold out the venues even
though we didn't have a record out. That fires us up again. On
the Gold Coast in Australia it was like Beatlemania. We received
rave reviews and could have sold the venues out three times over.'

On that tour last summer we were helped by the fact that the
radio stations responded to requests for UB40 by plucking our
version of the Police song 'Every Breath You Take' from the soundtrack to last year's American comedy movie *50 First Dates*.

When we got to Hawaii they expected us to play it because
it had been a massive local radio hit. What to do, since we hadn't
even rehearsed it? To try and knock together a live version on
the spot would have been short-changing the fans – you never
want to go out live with something that hasn't been worked out
precisely. So we discussed our options with the promoter and
eventually 'Every Breath You Take' was played over the sound

system right at the end of the show. The audience went nuts, and also went home happy.

After a career as long and productive as ours we have so much back catalogue to choose from, and it's sometimes difficult to know what to miss out from a set of twenty-odd songs. We are always mindful that fans have paid a lot of money to see us, and expect at the very least the two hardy perennials: 'Red Red Wine' and 'I Can't Help Falling in Love with You'. Everything else is a moveable feast, but we'll make sure there are some band as well as some crowd favourites. For example, 'Wear You to the Ball' will be in there so Astro can do his thing.

Not that he could come with us to Hawaii last year because he was done for herb cultivation, and even after three appeals they wouldn't let him into the States. In the event our production crew filmed him so that it looked like he was on stage with us. We're told that it looked good, but it didn't make up for a crucial element missing.

Before each tour Robin puts the sets together and then we all argue about what songs should feature in the show. But we all know that there is no point in giving the crowd tunes we want to hear. It's not about that. The audience comes first with UB40, and they're paying us to do what they've always paid us to do.

If you give an architect drawings for a two-up, two-down house and he comes back and tells you he's turned it into a castle, you're within your rights to be displeased. We think that pop stars who try out new and untested material on their audiences are arrogant if they don't at least play the tunes which elevated them to that position.

'I can honestly say, hand on heart, that I have never tired of performing "Red Red Wine", and at this rate I never will,' says Robin. 'It's all about the crowd response. On our own, in rehearsal, we don't bother doing it until the very last minute, and only then as a production run-through so the crew can get the lights and the other stuff right.

'But on stage, as soon as Ali goes into the first word of the song, the audience is up on its feet. You can't deny that response. Live performance is all about communication, and when the crowd is responding wildly, that's the ultimate communication, isn't it?'

Working off each other like a band again by playing live together in the studio has been inspiring and the enthusiasm had became infectious. It's as though the intervening two decades of studio wizardry and computer gadgetry hadn't existed.

On *Who You Fighting For?* we sound like UB40 once more, and, more importantly, our music sounds like reggae in its purest form. Just what our fans want from us. And every one of us is happy with the situation (we think!).

'These days we're working faster than ever,' says Ali. 'During the stint in the studio for the latest album we laid down basic backing tracks for forty-three songs.

'For a few weeks all we did was cut bass, drum and rhythm ideas, just like we used to. We soon had enough for several albums!'

The songs kept on coming. We recorded a wicked version of the Four Tops' classic. 'It's All in the Game' – which didn't actually make the cut but may well come out at some time in the future. Earl came up with the original bass pattern and we changed it to half time and reggaefied it. But there was such a wealth of new music we eventually shelved that.

In that atmosphere it became second nature to conjure out of the air a full new set of songs, including a couple of originals which Bill Curbishley saw immediately as dead-cert singles. There are also some covers: the version of the Manhattans' 'Kiss and Say Goodbye' was the first single off the album and came out this summer, while we have also done The Jamaicans' 'Things You Say You Love', Lennon and McCartney's 'I'll Be On My Way' and Matumbi's 'After Tonight', a tribute to the pioneering British reggae band who played at the Jug all those years ago when we ran our reggae night.

Everyone around the band, important people like our engineers, Danny Sprigg and Jamie Travers, Brian's son, were beside themselves with happiness, having endured the pulling-teeth sessions for the previous albums.

Danny and Jamie are very good for us. They have the right temperament and have lasted at DEP for several years, because they are so good at maintaining equilibrium and keeping on the ball while responding to the pressures from all eight of us. 'It takes devotion, which they have,' says Robin. 'They can't have off days or be arsing around like the rest of us. The vast majority of the band accept that a lot of work is done while they aren't in the studio, but I wonder sometimes whether they recognise exactly how much effort and skill is put in by people like Jamie and Dan.'

After years of arguing over whether we should do cover versions or not – because of the sniping in the press about our success being wholly based on covers – we made the conscious move of splitting the album 70:30 in favour of original tracks.

'I've written a song about my life with Julie called "One Woman Man", because that's what she has made me,' says Ali. 'And there's a song called "Reasons" – an idea of Ali's which I completed – which is about my relationship with Luci,' says Robin.

The new songs seemed to come out of nowhere and the time we were recording the album was a very exciting and creative period. 'With this album I was interested in writing about conflicts like Iraq and the propaganda machines that roll into action,' says Robin. 'That's why the title track asks the question Who You Fighting For? We're asking the squaddies whether they really understand what the conflict is about. It's also another way of saying: what side are you on?'

We're still talking politics, asking people like the squaddies: Don't you know what's going on? 'Burden of Shame', 'Present Arms', the songs we wrote years ago are about the same thing.

We've been asking the same questions for twenty-five years, but had our greatest success with cover versions of love songs, which gives a wrong public perception of us as writers. In interviews we are always asked: 'Why did you stop being political?' Our answer is: We never did.

On the other hand we've been dubbed 'the dour Campbell brothers' because of our political stance. But then when things like *Labour of Love* were released the critics asked: 'Why are you smiling and dancing all the time?' You can't win.

We know that we're on a hiding to nothing expecting to be played on Radio One. It came as a great shock to us when, after fifteen years of regular airplay, the changes at the station meant that we no longer get a look-in. But that's cool.

It would be a different story if we were seventeen or twenty-five, but Radio One is targeted at kids, and the 'tweenage' market of eight to twelve-year-olds who now buy music aren't the slightest bit interested in us. You've only got to watch *CD:UK* once to know we're not going to be on it.

In recent times UB40 has started to receive recognition from some quarters. A couple of years ago there was a *South Bank Show* dedicated to us and the story of reggae, which was a real tribute. We found Melvyn Bragg absolutely delightful. No attitude and not at all full of himself. He was genuinely pleasant and knew all about us, so his research team had obviously done their home-work. And he got passively, massively stoned just by hanging around us!

We're all different in the band, that's what makes us, and also what keeps us at each others' throats on occasion. Writing this book has brought home to us the unique chemistry with exists within this entity, UB40.

Astro, for instance, is the entertainer. He's contributing more then ever. It was very difficult for us to perform without him when he wasn't allowed into Hawaii last year. Even though technically it went without a hitch, we missed him like mad up there on stage.

Brian is a great lyricist, having written some of our best songs. 'I've said it before – "I Won't Close My Eyes" is my favourite UB40 song, and that's down to Brian,' says Ali. 'Mind you, some of the Brians I know are lovely; I've had a great time with them. As was once said of Mick Jagger, Brian is a lovely bunch of blokes!'

Jimmy, who is also a great lyricist, though not as prolific as Brian, has proven himself on our latest album. After twenty-five years he can still hold the beat down, so it's no surprise that all sorts of musicians – from Jamaican stars to the surprising likes of Primal Scream – big him up.

Earl is a great, great bassist. It was sad that it took him such a long time to halt all the one-finger keyboards and come back to playing again but he is back at the top of his form, helping us make some of our best reggae in years.

Mickey is the unsung hero of the band, not so much the Charlie Watts of UB40 as the Curly Watts! He's not the greatest keyboard player in the world, but he comes up with fantastic lines. Mickey is a unique character. The first time he went to Jamaica he travelled with a mate and stayed on the beach in Negril. We turned up a fortnight later and found his pal, who said he hadn't seen Mickey since the day they arrived. We went to the cottage and knocked on the door. It was opened by this thing, which looked more like a toffee crisp than our brother Mickey. He had been eaten alive by sandflies and mosquitoes and decided that the safest thing was to stay indoors. 'I don't understand what's going on,' he complained.

We got inside the cottage and everywhere, in every available space, was a mosquito coil. There was enough stock in there to open Mickey's Mosquito Coil Emporium. The only problem was that he hadn't lit even one of them – he thought that it was enough just to take them out of their packs!

Norman is the Rhythm Machine, the best live percussionist either of us has ever witnessed and played with. He had a tough upbringing and he has a mad personality, but you can count on Norman ('not to turn up to rehearsals,' says Ali). Norman has never changed and he is ultra-loyal. He's a good man to have in your corner.

We don't feel the need to have studios and recording gear at our homes. Why should we? We've got an entire set-up of our own in Birmingham. 'I've been offered loads of production jobs by all sorts of bands,' says Robin. 'But I've turned them all down because the only people I am interested in producing are UB40. That's all I care about.'

Whenever we have tried to bring in an outsider to work on production and mixing, we have always ended up at odds with them. It's far better for us to be at odds with each other, because the compromise achieved is between us. 'It is alien to me to give over the final say to somebody who has had nothing to do with actually making the music,' says Robin. 'It might only be two or three or four members of the band who are involved in the mixing process, but they are all working with UB40 in mind, towards a common aim. Our views often may be at odds, but in typical UBs style, they eventually dovetail together to create this sound which is uniquely our own.'

UB40 is a family which extends beyond the eight of us; some of the crew have stuck with the band through thick and thin. Our roadies Animal and Dougie have been with us since the days rehearsing in the Trafalgar Road basement, before we played our first gig.

Animal lived in one of the flats there, and was an apprentice toolmaker at the time. One evening he stuck his head round the door, intrigued by the racket we were making. Then he started to help out, humping our gear for no money. Months and months went by before we ever paid him a wage and at one point he rose to tour manager. Sadly Animal's dad died a few years back, so he took six months out and then came back and asked whether he could just be a roadie again. Here he is today, having travelled the world for twenty-five years and seen just about everything.

Roadies get a bad press but the good ones are special people.

'In a live situation you have to have faith that your roadie will move heaven and earth to fix whatever is wrong,' says Robin. 'The only time you notice the presence of a roadie is when something is not technically right.'

At one point Animal was Ali's roadie as his guitar tech, while Robin had Lloyd. He was a big strong guy and seemed indestructible back then, but sadly we lost him in 1997, a victim of the lifestyle. We still miss him.

There are other people like Carole Beirne in our office and Paul 'Wingy' Hunter, another of our crew, who are as much part of UB40 as the band members. They have worked for us for decades and know how to handle us but at the same time act like complete professionals.

There has been a downside to being in an internationally successful band. Only two members – Brian and Jimmy – are with the same partners after all these years. The rest of us have gone through the mill in terms of relationships, though out in the 'real world', how many out of eight guys would still be with the same person after twenty-five years?

It's also incredible to us that, midway through the first decade of the twenty-first century, racism is still as prevalent the world over, though it's played with a lot more subtlety than when we started out in the 70s. Astro can tell you stories about being refused entry to nightclubs in our home town because he has dreadlocks, while one time in Germany he and Robin were frozen out by the bar staff and locals in a bar, who muttered 'schwarze' until they left. 'I was absolutely boiling about it,' says Robin. 'Astro, who's had to live with racism all his life, was completely calm. "Couldn't give a fuck," is all he would say.'

There's a guy at Birmingham Airport who always targets Astro for a search whenever he flies back from travels abroad, while poor old Norman – because of his Arabic surname – is more often than not strip-searched these days.

'I remember turning up in Sweden and people in the streets

have been open-mouthed because here was this group of blokes which included a couple of dreads,' says Robin. 'One old couple literally jumped backwards in shock at the sight of dreadlocks when we walked into the hotel reception.'

Unfortunately some things change very slowly.

26

Homegrown

It's very important that DEP is still situated in the heart of where we come from. Even though Ali lives in Dorset these days and Robin is in Warwickshire, our work and creativity are still firmly rooted in Brum.

'Birmingham has been brilliant to us,' says Robin. 'On the whole the people here are so laid-back. They don't get in a tizzy when they see us, because we're "the lads" to them, the boys who made good. Quite often they will go out of their way not to treat us like VIPs, which is great, a very Brummie approach to fame.'

Birmingham has also given us autonomy, allowing us to develop away from the music business. In the 60s it made sense for people like the Beatles to gravitate to London, because that was the only place where the music business existed. But we came up at a time when labels, studios and bands had sprung up all over, not just the Midlands, but Manchester, Scotland, Liverpool and Dublin, wherever. That still didn't stop most of our contemporaries rushing to the Smoke, but we have never seen the advantage.

And why should we go? These days there's a lot of money

being ploughed into Broad Street and Brindley Place. It's become groovy, with the Armadillo, Harvey Nicks, the Selfridges Food Hall, all those places which make the old Bull Ring a shabby and dim distant memory.

'My favourite place in Birmingham always has been and still is Stratford Road,' says Ali. 'It's got the best baltis in the world, and Indian silk and sari shops and food markets. Stratford Road demonstrates how multicultural our home town is.'

We all used to live within a couple of miles of the city centre, that's how much we love it. 'My home in Balsall Heath was open house,' says Ali. 'There'd be people coming and going at all hours of the day and night, dropping by to say hi or hang out. Eventually we moved out, but most of us are still within striking distance, and I seem to spend the majority of my time here still.'

It's no surprise to us that Birmingham was such a strong contender for European Capital of Culture in 2008. Liverpool eventually won out, but hopefully we and UB40 as a whole have contributed to the regeneration, especially the development of the east side, the area around DEP.

Brian in particular was very active and helped us head up the campaign as ambassadors to get the media interested in relocating to the area. Birmingham Council have also been great to us in recent years, probably because they've started to realise how useful UB40 can be to them. The fact that we are still here and very much part of the city has probably spurred them on.

Now there are TV studios moving into the east side of the city. Central TV is on its way, as is Birmingham College. We also want to set up a foundation for musicians, the performing arts, technicians and engineers. We want people to know that, if you want to work in this business, you don't have to travel outside Birmingham. There is a hell of a lot of talent in this town.

We own the entire plot of land around DEP, which is ripe for redevelopment as a residential zone, so there is every chance that we will sell up and eventually move from our current base to ensure that is underway. We already have planning permission to build apartments here, and agreement with a developer is apparently on its way. Obviously that would be a big financial manoeuvre but after the topsy-turvy fortunes of the band, we've always looked upon it as our pension.

If it all goes ahead and we do move, rest assured that DEP won't be shifting too far. Inner-city Birmingham is the spiritual and literal home of UB40 which could be why our music speaks to inner-city dwellers the world over.

Maybe staying here has allowed us to remain big fish in a little pond, but we are a Brummie band, and, to a certain extent, being rooted here has made us.

That's why we were never tempted to move to America, which is the usual route for bands who become successful there. We have spent a hell of a lot of time in the US, probably visiting every state in the union several times over.

'After the *Promises and Lies* tour I nearly bought a house in Florida,' confesses Robin. 'But eventually I realised that would be folly.

'To us America is still Babylon, always will be. It is a stunning country, with everything from deserts to mountains, but no matter how beautiful and varied the landscape, there isn't anything which would allow us to live too far from home.'

27

Who You Fighting For?

Getting on for three decades after we made our first tentative musical moves, not knowing whether we wanted to be a strictly dub band or 'jazz-dub-reggae', we feel that we have achieved what we set out to do: help to get global recognition for reggae. These days, on both the east and west coasts of America and even in parts of the heartland of the Midwest, it is embraced as much as rock, pop or hip-hop. In fact rap has really made the difference: so many of the biggest hits have utilised the samples and rhythms of Jamaica. Some of the UBs' kids are already involved – Ali Jr and Brian's son Jamie for example – while a lot of the others are very interested in making music.

'Obviously they have our full support, and probably a better chance than some of getting into the business,' says Robin. 'They, of anybody, will be aware of the cut-throat, hit-and-miss nature of this business.'

Both of Robin's kids are keen on music. 'I've always encouraged them to follow their dreams and would support them in whatever they wanted to do with their lives,' he says. 'It may sound clichéd but if there's one thing I've discovered about life after all these years, it's that it is not about the money. I know it may sound easy for me to say that, because I am comfortably off, but once you have money you realise that there are better goals to go for.'

Creatively, we've hit another peak. 'Musically, UB40's music went downhill after *Guns in the Ghetto* in 1997,' believes Ali. 'With hindsight we can see that albums like *Cover Up* weren't really up to scratch. Quite a few of the band members didn't really care enough, and that's always going to have an impact. But now we're riding high again.'

Our grandad once summed up the common thread that runs through the music made by the generations of the Campbells: 'All our music is a reflection of a social consciousness. We tend to choose, write and perform songs which have something to say about contemporary reality. Our songs are designed to help you to cope with life rather than help you to escape from it, which is what pop music does.'

Grandad has a point, but we realise that it is the differences between us brothers which have helped us survive in the same band together for twenty-five years, rather than the similarities.

What do we think of each other? That's a difficult one for brothers to sum up at the best of times, isn't it? Obviously we love each other, but having worked together so closely and so publicly has added layer upon layer of complexity to our relationship.

'Robin still drives the job, in the same way as he did as a presser at Leyland, working that anvil or whatever it was a quarter of a century ago,' believes Ali. 'He's crucial, because the sound of his and my voice together *IS* the sound of UB40.

'Apart from that, I do believe he is the worst-dressed man in pop, still wearing his slim-line Italian dancing pumps and rolling the sleeves of his shirt back like he did when he was a suede-head!'

Robin's response is: 'Young man, wear your size!'

Fraternal jibing aside, Robin pays tribute to Ali's bravery and skill. 'If we'd both been like me, UB40 wouldn't have existed, because we wouldn't have had Ali's talent,' says Robin. 'I love doing harmonies and building a vocal sound around his lead vocal. He is so good that as long as he's around I'll be backing him.'

On the other hand, if we'd both been like Ali, the band would most likely have fallen apart a long time ago!

'Make no mistake, UB40 would never have existed if it wasn't for Ali,' says Robin. 'Not only was he the catalyst, but he was the reason I was interested. If Earl, Jimmy and Brian, say, had asked me to be in their band I'd have said: "No thanks."

'But when Ali said: "We're serious", I believed him, particularly since he was prepared to put his compensation money into it. Having a few thousand quid back then was like having a fortune.

'We've said it before in this book but it really does all go back to us as kid brothers, dreaming of being Birmingham's answer to the Jackson Five. He was going to be the lead singer and I would be harmonising to his voice. I really hoped that Duncan would be in the band as well, because the three of us have the brother blend, a great vocal sound. We share a similarity of tonality and harmonics.

'But that wasn't to be because Duncan didn't take it seriously at the time, just didn't think it would happen.'

But it did and sometimes we still look at each other and ponder what exactly happened, though it never does to question these things too deeply. It has been a long, strange journey from a freezing cold basement with the toilet overflowing in Trafalgar Road to playing for Nelson Mandela.

We think about our grandfather, active on the unemployment marches during the Great Depression, singing his heart out with our nan. We think about his valour in fighting the bosses and then bringing his young family down from Scotland to the cold, grey, post-war Midlands.

We think about our own father making revolutionary moves of his own but in the sphere of music, rubbing shoulders with the likes of Dylan and Paul Simon, while Mom not only tended home to an unruly bunch of kids but also espoused liberal ideas and common sense at a time when it ran against the grain to believe in equality and fairness.

Then there's us, on the face of it the most unlikely success stories of the post-punk era: Robin a Leyland fitter and Ali an unemployed dope-smoking layabout. But we always knew we had something. It wasn't just the fire that propelled Grandad and our father, but something special to ourselves: the love of the sound of the streets, black music, reggae music. And we achieved what we set out to do: to show that the throb of inner-city Balsall Heath had, and still has, global appeal.

'Ali and I thought we'd be grandads together, chuckling about the time we dreamt of having a band,' says Robin. 'Ali made that a reality, and sometimes – even to this day – I pinch myself to think that it all came true.'

Index

The line begins here.

All UB40 songs and albums are indexed under UB40.

copyright, sued for breach 110
and drugs 126–37; avoidance of
    hard drugs 73; habits
    increase 85–9, 124–5; raided
    for drugs in Seychelles
    129–31; some members cut
    out for health reasons 171
DVDs 166
and films: *Speed 2* 141
formation 46–55
gigs: early 56–64; Free Nelson
    Mandela 115; Police support
    gig in Fréjus 128–9; Teenage
    Cancer Trust 187; sets and
    songs 191
in Ireland rehearsing 184
managers: take on Woods 57;
    split with Woods 80–1; Dave
    Campbell takes over as
    manager 81; part with Dave
    Campbell 83; replace
    Freedman with Harper 113;
    break with Harper 156–7;
    appoint Curbishley 186
and MI5 82–3
and money: wealth 138–40;
    finacial problems 157–9
and overseas performance
    money 102
and politics 47–8, 82–3, 193–4
and producers and engineers
    69–70, 101, 193
production 196
and racism 197–8
and radio airplay policies
    166–7, 189, 194
record labels and distributors:
    signed to *Graduate* 64–6; split
    with Graduate 79–80; form

own record label and sign
    with CBS 83; let go by CBS
    89; sign with Virgin 89
roadies and team members 196
songwriting 68
studios: set up The Abattoir
    101, 103
tours: 1979 London tour 70–1;
    Pretenders' support tour
    71–3; 1980 European tour
    75; 1981 Australian tour 90;
    1982 African tour 90–3;
    1983 US tour 93; 1986
    Soviet tour 93–5; tour
    dangers 96–7; 1990s South
    American tour 98; Sri
    Lankan tour 98–9;
    economics 114; 1988–89
    world tour 113–20; destruc-
    tive effect 122–5; *Guns in the
    Ghetto* tour called off 157;
    Labour of Love III tour
    163–6; atmosphere on buses
    168; 2004 Hawaii tour
    190–1
troublemaking reputation 74–5
TV performances: debut 73;
    first *Top of the Pops* perform-
    ance 62, 74; *South Bank
    Show* 194
USA breakthrough 116–17
UB40: SONGS AND ALBUMS
'After Tonight' 192
Baggariddim 111
The Best of – Vol. I 111
'Breakfast in Bed' 107
'Bring Me Your Cup' 177
'Broken Windows' 51
'Burden of Shame' 68, 80